Praise for
Life's Missing Instruction Manual

"In a world of confusion and stress, it's a relief and a joy to have this book to read and give to family and friends."

> —Jack Canfield, co-creator, #1 *New York Times* best-selling Chicken Soup for the Soul® series; author, *The Success Principles* ™

"Every man, woman, and child ought to study this book like a scientist. Every high school, college, and graduate school ought to include it in their curriculum. Joe Vitale reveals and reminds us of the wisdom it takes to be happy, healthy, and wealthy.

"I couldn't put this book down."

> —Steve Siebold, author, *177 Mental Toughness Secrets of the World Class*

"Brilliant, simple and profound. If we could all absorb and live by just one of these lessons every day, our lives would truly be abundant. As I read, I realized I needed about 50 copies to give to the people I love and care about. This is truly a unique work of art from the spirit of a beautiful man. *Life's Missing Instruction Manual* will make you think, feel, and be more curious than ever about what you can create for your life and for those you love."

> —Wendi Friesen, CEO and founder, www.Wendi.com

"Joe Vitale opens the wisdom of the ages to all who will read the pages of this winsome, precious gem of a book. The missing manual may be the only self-help book anyone really needs, if they would simply heed it. What a gift to the world it is!"

> —Marcus L. Gitterle, MD, wellness consultant, nutraceutical designer

"This is a fabulous book! I suggest you buy multiple copies so you can give them to your friends. They will appreciate it."

> —Cindy Cashman, million-selling author

"Wow! This book is the simplest, clearest explanation of how to live life to the fullest that I have ever come across, and having co-founded HealthyWealthynWise.com, I've seen hundreds! Joe is right, they should pass this book out to everyone just after birth. Snip! The cord gets cut and they hand you your own copy!"

—**Ric Thompson, HealthyWealthynWise.com**

"This new book by Dr. Joe Vitale is ripe with wisdom that will nourish and enrich the mind and soul of any who choose to feast on its words. It is an essential book for every person to guide them through life."

—**Dr. Rick Barrett, author, *Dare to Break through the Pain*, www.healedbymorning.com**

"This is the volume that should have come tucked under the pillow in your bassinet—words of wisdom about life, and yes, about business, too. Once again, Joe Vitale speaks directly to those of us who seek success through spirituality."

—**Jillian Coleman Wheeler, www.GrantMeRich.com**

"This book is so good I'm reading it to my sons and they love it, too. It's a lifetime of wisdom delivered in quick, easy-to-digest lessons everyone really should have at birth."

—**Craig Perrine, www.MaverickMarketer.com**

"Joe did it again! He delivers the secrets to living a healthier happier life in easy-to-read nuggets of wisdom and parables. The perfect gift book for you and everyone else who wants a better life."

—**Nerissa Oden, http://TheVideoQueen.com**

Life's *Missing* Instruction Manual

**The Guidebook
You Should Have
Been Given
at Birth**

JOE VITALE

WILEY

John Wiley & Sons, Inc.

Published by John Wiley & Sons, Inc., Hoboken, New Jersey.
Published simultaneously in Canada.

Cover Design: Paul McCarthy
Cover Photograph: © Steve Cole

Limit of Liability/Disclaimer of Warranty: While the publisher and author have used their best efforts in preparing this book, they make no representations or warranties with respect to the accuracy or completeness of the contents of this book and specifically disclaim any implied warranties of merchantability or fitness for a particular purpose. No warranty may be created or extended by sales representatives or written sales materials. The advice and strategies contained herein may not be suitable for your situation. You should consult with a professional where appropriate. Neither the publisher nor author shall be liable for any loss of profit or any other commercial damages, including but not limited to special, incidental, consequential, or other damages.

For general information on our other products and services or for technical support, please contact our Customer Care Department within the United States at (800) 762-2974, outside the United States at (317) 572-3993 or fax (317) 572-4002.

Wiley also publishes its books in a variety of electronic formats. Some content that appears in print may not be available in electronic books. For more information about Wiley products, visit our web site at www.wiley.com.

Library of Congress Cataloging-in-Publication Data:
Vitale, Joe.
    Life's missing instruction manual : the guidebook you should have been given at birth / Joe Vitale.
        p. cm.
    ISBN-13: 978-0-471-76849-4 (cloth : alk. paper)
    ISBN-10: 0-471-76849-9 (cloth : alk. paper)
    1. Life skills—Handbooks, manuals, etc.   I. Title.
    HQ2037.V58 2006
    158—dc22

                                                                    2005026007

Printed in the United States of America.

10   9   8   7   6   5   4   3

"Honor all life."

BENU

CONTENTS

External Connections: Caring for Others in Your Life

Troubleshooting: Taking Care of Yourself

Optimum Performance: Getting the Best Out of Your Life

Specifications: What You Need to Know About Others

FOREWORD

*ow rare it is in life to discover a book in which every idea is sound and every word rings true! That is exactly what I was privileged to discover in Joe Vitale's new book, *Life's Missing Instruction Manual*. I predict that you, too, will feel a deep appreciation for Joe's contribution when you take to heart the treasure trove of practical enlightenment in this book. There's something valuable to learn on every page.

One of the vows I made to myself and the universe when I began writing books of my own was that I would never write about any technique or principle that I had not personally found practical and useful in my own life. It is clear from reading *Life's Missing Instruction Manual* that Joe Vitale has taken a similar vow. I believe it's a particularly important one in today's media-rich environment, in which much bull is slung in the name of truth. Thirty-some years ago, when I was working on my doctorate in Counseling Psychology at Stanford, I had grown disenchanted at encountering one expert after another who had no personal experience with the processes he or she advocated. The excuse usually given was that it was important to maintain clinical detachment. The message was always "Do as I say, not as I do." The wisdom that Joe dispenses in this book comes from the opposite end of the spectrum. There is, thankfully, no clinical detachment here; rather, there is the distilled practical wisdom from a life lived on the front lines, helping real people solve real problems.

As I read the bite-sized bits of wisdom in the *Manual*, I found myself thinking over and over, "I've said this exact same thing to therapy clients!" In working with more than 20,000 individual clients and nearly 4,000 couples during the past 25 years, my wife and I have learned the useful truth of the nuggets of wisdom Joe reveals. Sometimes we learned them the hard way, by doing the opposite first, and my fondest hope for this book is that it will save readers the painful trouble of having to learn some of these lessons by experience.

One of my early heroes, Buckminster Fuller, valued highly making mistakes. He said that one of the main reasons he kept his creativity flourishing throughout his long life was that he made more mistakes than any other person he'd ever met. If you listened closely to Bucky's understanding of mistakes, though, it was clear that he did not even believe in them. What he called mistakes were really life-lessons he could learn from. It's our openness to learning that keeps us from repeating life-lessons over and over. Increase your openness to learning, Bucky would say, and you keep making higher and higher quality of mistakes.

It's clear from reading this manual that Joe Vitale has learned a great deal from life. He articulates his learning with brilliant simplicity, so that each of us who reads his wisdom can immediately put it into play. In addition, this is a fun book to read. As one who gets several hundred books a year sent to him for endorsements (99 percent of which I must say no to), I appreciate the fun factor that Joe weaves into the deep wisdom of the book. All in all, *Life's Missing Instruction Manual* is a wise, useful, and entertaining contribution, one which I recommend with enthusiasm to anyone who seeks a deeper, richer experience of life.

—Gay Hendricks, Ph.D.
Author of *Conscious Living, The Corporate Mystic* and
(with Dr. Kathlyn Hendricks) *Conscious Loving*
Co-Founder, The Spiritual Cinema Circle and
The Transformational Book Circle

ACKNOWLEDGMENTS

The idea for this book came from Matt Holt, my editor and now dear friend at John Wiley & Sons, Inc., publishers. I'm honored he came to me with it. My assistant, Suzanne Burns, helped me pull it all together and kept me relatively sane during the writing process. Mark Weisser contributed editorial feedback. My Master Mind group offered support throughout the writing process: Craig Perrine, Cindy Cashman, Pat O'Bryan, Bill Hibbler, Nerissa Oden, and Jillian Coleman-Wheeler. Nerissa, my love, kept the cats and Wolfie fed so I could focus on writing. Many people contributed articles and ideas to the book, and they are acknowledged throughout. Also, thanks to the staff at John Wiley & Sons, Inc. for making this book a work of art, including Shannon Vargo, Kate Lindsay, and Kevin Holm. If I've missed anyone, I apologize. I am very grateful for the team effort and very impressed with the final result. Thank you, everyone.

INTRODUCTION

~

How to Use This Manual

INTRODUCTION

What you do now creates your future.

—DR. JOE VITALE

Many years ago, maybe 20 years ago, I found an unusual hand-sewn manual from Florence, Italy. It consisted of mostly blank pages of handmade paper, in a genuine leather book, tan in color. It was the kind of rare antique you could imagine Leonardo da Vinci sketching in. Or Michelangelo. Or maybe where a wise old wizard noted his insights into how the universe worked.

I spent years writing notes in this magical little book. Not diary entries so much as life discoveries. This was my way of keeping track of what I was learning as I explored life. Some of my ideas and discoveries ended up in one of my earlier books, *The Attractor Factor*.

But I didn't reveal all the secrets in my previous book, as I felt they were in many respects too overwhelming for the average person to grasp, let alone use. I also wasn't sure I could fully explain the advanced concepts. So I kept many of the notes to myself.

I never intended to publish this material. If I had, I would have typed my insights, not handwritten them, and I certainly would have written more legibly. But there you have it. One of the unfolding lessons in life is you never know what lies around the next corner. The thing you do today, thinking it is for no one but you, could become the thing the public buys, reads, and uses to change how they live.

That said, here are the musings of a man in his middle years. (I hope these are my middle years.) I have much more to learn (which suggests a second volume sometime down the road). But maybe the enclosed will save *you* some time and trouble along the way.

Also, since I don't know it all (yes, I'm surprised, too), I have asked others to contribute some of their own life lessons to this manual. You'll find them throughout the book.

Enjoy.

—Dr. Joe Vitale
www.mrfire.com

YOU

~

Congratulations on Your Life

Your Point of Power Is Now

War.

Economic concerns.

Poor business.

Unemployment.

It sure looks bad, doesn't it?

But I also want to remind you that we have lived, survived, and prospered through far worse times. For example:

In 1780 George Washington said, "We are without money; and have been so for a great length of time. . . ."

He went on to create an estate worth three-quarters of a million dollars when he died.

In 1840 a traveler wrote, "So great is the panic, and so dreadful the distress, that there are a great many farms prepared to receive crops, and some of them actually planted, and yet deserted, not a human being to be found upon them."

But we got over that problem, too.

In 1857 an editorial stated, "It is a gloomy moment in history. Not for many years—not in the lifetime of most men who read this newspaper—has there been so much grave and deep apprehension."

That passed, as well.

In 1873 this country had a panic that shook the nation. A newspaper wrote:

"All over the country manufacturers are closing their works and discharging their operatives, simply because they can neither sell the goods they make nor borrow money to carry them until the demand for them revives."

Yet we survived that panic, too.

In 1893 one man wrote of the troubling times he saw: "I have been through all the panics of the last thirty years, but I have

7

never seen one in which the distress was so widespread and reached so many people who had previously not been affected as this panic of 1893."

And we got through that one, too.

We also got through the Great Depression of 1929, two World Wars, the Y2K panic, and even 9-11.

What appears to be gloom and doom is often just the focus of the media. Consider what Gandhi once said: "When I despair, I remember that all through history the ways of truth and love have always won. There have been tyrants, and murderers, and for a time they can seem invincible, but in the end they always fall. Think of it . . . always."

I could go on and on. The point is this: Life will always have ups and downs. The secret is to flow with the tide as best we can. Complaining about what is keeps you from spotting or even creating new opportunities. In every panic, in every generation, men and women with eyes wide open saw and seized opportunities.

Whether it was George Washington who went on to become president and build his own fortune, or P.T. Barnum who went on to prosper during the Civil War, the fact remains: Circumstances don't make you, you make you. This "bad time" might become the greatest period of prosperity for you.

Maybe you just have to relax your demands. In 1941 Bruce Barton wrote, "I have been out of a job three times in my life. Each time I made a survey of my surroundings and discovered that there was work to be done, though not the same kind of work I had been doing."

Barton was a best-selling author, Congressman, popular speaker, and founder of one of the largest advertising agencies in the world, BBDO. He also became a millionaire.

And don't fall for the trap that the past was better than the present. In 1907 the famous tycoon John D. Rockefeller said: "People sometimes talk as if we older men lived in a day of peculiar opportunity, as if there were no chance today for a young man to do what has been done by my generation of men, as if all the avenues were closed, all the big things done. Nothing could be more mistaken.

Why, the time in which I opened my eyes was a midnight of darkness, and this is blazing noon."

A word to the wise: Listen, act, and prosper.

There are opportunities around you.

Which will you see first and act on now?

The point of power in your life is now.

This moment is your time of blazing noon.

❧

"I Wish I Had Learned . . ."
Jim Edwards

"I wish I had learned that I can do anything I really believe I can do. It may sound simple, but it's the basis of any and all achievement (or lack thereof) in anyone's life. As soon as I believed I could, I could . . . and before that, I believed I couldn't, and I couldn't. If you want to change your life for the better, change your belief about what's possible for you, what you're entitled to, and what you can accomplish if you simply put your mind to it. Sure, it sounds obvious, but until you live it, breath it, and make it a part of who you are as a person, you'll just keep getting what you've gotten in the past, which I'll bet isn't what you want. Start believing in yourself and your world will change for the better faster than you ever dreamed possible!"

———

Jim Edwards, author *5 Steps To Getting Anything You Want* www.HowToGetAnythingYouWant.com.

❧

You Can Be Happy Now

No one will believe you when you tell them this, but happiness is a choice.

You can be happy right now.

Yes, right now.

How?

With the decision to be happy.

You don't need more money (though it would be nice).

You don't need to be thinner (though you might like it).

You don't need anything (though you might still want things).

You can simply say, "I'm going to be happy right now."

This is the trick few know because they didn't have the owner's manual for their life.

Smile. Be happy.

"If you're not happy, you're missing a great opportunity."

                                         ∽

Life Doesn't Have to Be Hard

Life doesn't have to be hard.

Few know this (unless they've read this manual, too).

Most people think they need to fight and struggle. Not so. You can let life unfold. The secret is to focus on what you want, do what is before you to make it happen, and trust the process.

Yes, life can be hard.

But it can also be easy.

Most of the difference is in how you look at what is happening.

If you regard running a marathon as hard, you won't find it very easy. But if you enjoy running and consider a marathon a personal challenge you welcome, then you will regard running it as easy. Yes, you may sweat and struggle and pant along the way, but you'll enjoy it.

As with everything else, the choice is yours.

                                         ∽

You Are Behind Your Eyes

I was on my back on the doctor's operating table. It was minor surgery, so I was awake as the doc dug into my chest, cutting, snipping, cleaning a wound I had.

It was no big deal. Not heart surgery or a lung transplant. Yet I lay on that table, wide awake, and felt as if he were working on a machine. I just happened to be *in* the machine. What he was doing wasn't happening to me but to something I owned.

Take note:

You have a body.

But you are not your body.

You have a mind.

But you are not your mind.

You have emotions.

But you are not your emotions.

You are the being behind it all, able to choose what you want, able to direct it all.

Choose wisely. (The rest of this manual will help.)

Your Feelings Are Hidden Thoughts

"Feelings are shadows of thoughts," wrote Michael Ryce in his book, *Why Is This Happening to Me . . . Again?*

Your thoughts create your feelings, but sometimes it happens at such lightning fast speed that you don't hear the thoughts as they whiz into a feeling.

"Your feelings inform you of the nature of the impact of the energy of your thoughts on your physiology," writes Ryce. "If you are in pain, you are the one in error."

Become aware.

This concept will become clearer as you review this manual and live your life. For now, realize that your feelings aren't sneaking up on you unannounced, and they are not unavailable to your control.

Your feelings are from your thoughts. Change your thoughts, and you'll change your feelings.

This will take some getting used to.

Enjoy the process.

❦

Everything Is Energy Directed by Your Thoughts

Energy makes up your entire world—you, me, this book, the chair you're sitting on, the room you're in, and so on.

How you think begins to organize energy into form.

For example, hold a negative thought in your mind for a few minutes and then go look in the mirror. You'll see darkness around you. You'll probably have slumped shoulders, droopy eyes, and a frown. Your thought created the changes, which others will perceive as an energy change.

Now hold a positive thought for a few minutes. Go look in the mirror. You'll see brightness. Your shoulders will be square, eyes twinkling, and a smile on your face. Again, your thought changed your energy.

Thoughts begin to change the energy of everything around you. Hold positive thoughts to help yourself, and others, lead happy, productive lives.

❦

You Can't Stop Your Thoughts but You Don't Have to Listen to Them, Either

Your mind will keep working night and day, awake and asleep, throughout your life.

Good thing, too. You need it to help you walk, talk, drive, and live.

But along the way you'll notice some thoughts make you feel good, and other thoughts make you feel bad. Some thoughts will be good; others will be bad. Some thoughts will encourage positive behavior; others may encourage negative behavior.

You don't have to obey all your thoughts.

A T-shirt I bought years ago had this saying printed on it: "Meditation is not what you think."

Exactly.

Meditation is that space *behind* your thoughts. The more you can pay attention to the screen where the thoughts appear, the more liberated you will be of them.

This may not make sense right now, so just remember this:

"You can't stop your thoughts but you don't have to listen to them, either."

∽

Everything Is a Projection from Inside You

You'll find this hard to believe at first, but everything in your life is a projection from the shadow side of your own mind.

I told you this would be hard to grasp.

Blame and excuses are easy. They let you avoid responsibility.

But your life is all about total responsibility.

When you look around, all you notice is seen within your own mind. How it got there is from your own mental filters. To change anything, you must change the inside.

This is difficult to understand because most people don't have this manual. They were never told that life happens from the inside out.

When someone upsets you, they pushed a button within you.

When a situation occurs that you don't like, it was drawn to you from your inside programming.

If this is true (and it is), how do you change it?

You have to own the fact that you attracted it.

All of it.

You then have to accept the inside of you and release it.

So if someone upset you, look at how you upset yourself, love it, and let it go. As you change your inner self, you will find the outer change.

This is a big principle.

Sit with it.

∿

Your Nature Is Your Current Act

When I was in college, a friend of mine said I was naturally pessimistic. He noted my sadness, the glum look on my face, my constant complaining, and he concluded that pessimism was my nature.

Thirty years later I was interviewed on a radio show, and the host wanted to know why my nature was so optimistic. She noted my smile, the light in my eyes, my constant exclaims of gratitude, and concluded optimism was my nature.

Well, which was my nature?

Both were.

Your nature is simply a role you play, based on your choices. Change your choices and you change your act. Do it long enough and it will seem like your nature.

Wally Mintos, in *The Results Book*, wrote: "When you haven't got your role completely memorized, then you feel like you're acting. When you have the role memorized and it becomes a habit, you think it's your nature."

If you want to change your nature, start acting in a new way. At first it may seem awkward, as if you are truly acting. After a while it will become second nature, and everyone will assume you were born that way.

∿

How to Know What You Want

Some people say they don't know what they want.

They're lying.

You always know what you want. You may not want to admit it, though, not even to yourself.

When you state what you want, you then either have to start making it happen or you have to start making excuses for it not happening.

Sometimes it's just easier to say you don't know what you want.
But that's a lie.
You do know.
So admit it.
No one is looking.
No one is listening.
So what do you want?

⌘

You Get More of
Whatever You Focus on

People without this manual focus on what they don't want. They get more of it.

You're smarter than that. (Right?)

If you want wealth, focus on wealth.

If you want health, focus on health.

If you want happiness, focus on happiness.

It's an overlooked but guaranteed secret of the universe: You get more of whatever you focus on.

⌘

Whatever You Say after "I Am"
Defines Who You Become

An important lesson is realizing that you create yourself by whatever you say after the words, "I am."

I'm not talking about the words you speak out loud, though that is part of it. I'm referring to the words you say in the privacy of your own mind.

"I am fat" or "I am stupid" may sound like assessments of who you are now. Actually, they are the commands that led you to your current reality.

Begin declaring who you want to become and soon the words will become facts.

❧

What You Love or What You Hate Will Be Drawn to You

This is the law of attraction at work, but basically, what you love or what you hate will be drawn to you.

In other words, if you truly hate a political party or a way of life, you will find it everywhere. Your hate is an intense energy which will attract more of the same energy.

By the same token, if you truly love something, whether a car or an activity, you will tend to draw more of it into your experience.

The lesson is to choose your passions carefully. Knowing that you control the magnet will help awaken you to your own power.

❧

Your Body Requires No Assembly

Take a look in the mirror.

Everything accounted for?

Got some arms? Legs? Eyes? Ears?

Some people come with incomplete parts, but they can still have a terrific life. So don't worry about anything if your parts look small, or big, or are missing.

You're still OK.

If you have a thingy, you're a boy.

If you don't, you're a girl.

Either way, congratulations.

You have what you need to have a good life.

No assembly required, either.

❧

Great Hair, Great Day

My late ex-wife loved make-up and hair styling. Her business card contained the one-line statement that said it all: "Great hair, great day."

The lesson here is to feel good about yourself. If that means nice hair or a nice shirt, so be it. The better you feel, the more the world will respond to you in kindness.

Your Memory Will Never Be Accurate

You won't remember everything.

You won't remember anything accurately.

The best thing to do is take notes.

When I spoke at an event in San Antonio on marketing, one of the greatest marketers of all time was in the audience. He was Ted Nicholas, one of my heroes and mentors. I noticed that Ted took notes furiously and copiously throughout my presentation.

When I spoke at an event in Las Vegas, Jack Canfield, creator of the Chicken Soup idea, which became a series of bestselling books, was in the audience. He, too, took pages of notes.

Neither of these legends had bad memories or lacked in success. Yet they knew the value in taking notes. It helped them solidify what they were learning. And it helped them have records to review later, so they could refresh themselves of what they absorbed.

In life, our mind will play tricks. You think you'll remember things—even the key secrets in this very manual—but you'll forget them within hours. And if you do recall them, you'll have reinterpreted them with your own spin.

Take notes.

Love

Love will cause you to become disoriented in the most delightful way.

Enjoy it. It will last longer if you commit to it and not run from it.

Love of people, pets, places, and even things is natural.

When you are near the end of your life, you will look back at all that you loved and you will smile.

Sex

You'll want it.

You'll like it.

Find someone who likes to play the same way you do, and enjoy.

Sex isn't bad.

Sex isn't dirty.

Sex without love is acrobatics.

Sex with love is bliss.

Food

Your machine/body requires high octane food.

It needs it every three hours.

Not much, though.

A little protein, a lot of vegetables and fruits, plenty of water, and you're set.

Warning: Eating food as a social activity is deceptive. You don't need the extra fuel. Take in too much and your machine will get larger than your garage may be able to park.

Exercise

You must exercise.

Your body is the vehicle that carries you around for your life. It needs maintenance. Moving your body keeps it running smoothly.

Exercise doesn't have to be hard.

Gentle exercises, like yoga, are just as valuable as intense exercises, like rugby.

The idea is to enjoy the exercise you choose.

Exercise doesn't have to take long, either.

Do something every day for 30 minutes.

The other $23\frac{1}{2}$ hours are yours to do as you please.

I've managed to lose over 70 pounds in 8 months, keep it off, enter four fitness contests, and never miss a day of exercise. If I can do it after 50 years of struggling with obesity, you can do it, too.

⌒∾

Three Life Lessons I Wish I Had Learned Earlier
Dr. Paul Hartunian

When I look back, there are three lessons I've learned, each of which has become solidly hardwired into my psyche.

1. There never was anything to be afraid of. The opportunities I passed up, the people I never approached, the rock star I never became. All sacrificed at the altar of fear—fear that never really existed.

2. My worst decisions and actions happened when I was being petty, weak, or self-involved; when I made less-than-kind comments about people; when negative outside influences affected me.

3. I am on this planet for bigger purposes than accumulating riches. Thirteen years ago my life was permanently, profoundly altered by a dog named Milo. He put me on an entirely different life path. Milo helped me see that one of the major reasons I've been fortunate enough to accumulate substantial wealth is to use that money to help homeless, abused, and abandoned dogs.

Milo also taught me humility. As I stand on a platform, having just finished giving a 90-minute talk to an audience of hundreds, getting a standing ovation from the admiring crowd and getting a paycheck equal to many people's annual salary, I clearly keep in mind that at the same time on the next day I'll be back in my yard, cleaning up dog poop left by the dozen rescue dogs now in my care.

Thank you Milo.

———

Dr. Paul Hartunian is a famous speaker, author, and publicity expert. Read his free e-zine *Million Dollar Publicity Tactics* and learn how to get free publicity on radio and TV, in newspapers and magazines anywhere in the world. Go to: http://www.Hartunian.com/ezine

INTERNAL CAPABILITIES

❦

Understanding Your Life's Potential

Anything Is Possible

The vast majority of people have no idea that they control their experience. Their mindset is that of a victim. It's easy to blame and shirk responsibility on this level. It's okay. We all have to start someplace.

The next level up starts to play with the notion that life can be another way. You begin to entertain the idea that you can have, do, or be more.

Another level up from that is where you begin to take on the belief that we're not sure what is impossible. You play with the idea that life can be better, and maybe even great, and maybe even *your* life can be better and great.

And another level up from that you know that anything is possible. You take on the mental power of a deity. You begin to realize that anything—anything—is truly possible. The only limits are your own mental ones.

Go for the higher level.

Anything is possible.

You Create Your Future with a Pen

The secret of the ages is that you can create your future with a pen and your imagination.

Here's how:

Take out paper or turn on your computer. Pretend it is one year from today. Write a letter to a friend as if you have accomplished all that you wanted to accomplish. Go into detail. Feel the joyous emotions. Share your thrill as you detail your success.

This one single act, which you can do as often as you want, can command the universe to bring you what you need to make it your new reality.

It begins right now, with a pen.

Achieving Your Goals Is Easy

How to achieve your goals easily:

You must know what you want.
You must feel it as if it is already achieved.
You must do the next thing before you to achieve it.

That's it.
Easy, isn't it?

Your Mind Operates under Its Own Conception

"Mind operates under its own conception of itself."

Better read that again.

The statement was made by A.K. Mozumdar. I have no idea who he is or where he is. I read the line in the book *Prosperity Plus* by John Seaman Garns.

What does the quote mean?

Whatever you choose to believe, will be the concept that runs your mind.

What are you thinking right now, in response to reading the concept, "Mind operates under its own conception of itself"?

Whatever your answer, *that* is your current conception—and it is running your mind.

Are you happy with what you are thinking?

Get away from the dream that you are but the effect of something and know you are Cause Itself!
—FRANCES LARIMER WARNER,
Our Invisible Supply: Part 2. 1909

❧

How to Feel Better in One Minute

Life doesn't have to get you down. There's a secret to feeling better, and within one minute.

Here it is: Breathe slowly, deeply, completely, and sigh.

Here's how to do it:

Take in a deep breath. Feel your lungs.

Hold it for a few seconds.

Release it with a long, slow sigh of relief.

Do it again.

If necessary, repeat.

The release of oxygen will help you release any stuck mood.

❧

A Smile Is Universally Understood

No matter where you go, or what language people may speak, everyone in all cultures and countries understands and responds to a smile.

When we were in Italy, and ran into people who did not speak English, we could always smile and create a connection with the other person.

When you are walking down the street, and see a stranger, a smile can cause them to feel better—about you, their world, their day.

A smile is universally understood.

Use it openly and often.

It makes people curious.

꧁

Exercise: Laugh Like a Child with Milk Coming Out Your Nose

Laugh.

Do it right now.

Start laughing. Fake it at first. Push it. Then note how it starts to roll on its own. It takes on a movement of its own.

Laugh three times a day. Deep belly laughs. Do it in traffic. In bed. In the shower. Everywhere.

Even right now.

Do you need a reason?

That's funny all by itself.

You can laugh without reason.

Go ahead.

Show me.

꧁

Your Language Can Create Attractors

Don't swear.

When you swear, you send out a negative vibration that tends to attract more negativity.

Keep your word.

When you say you will do something and don't do it, you teach others (including yourself) that you cannot be trusted.

Watch how your words become reality.

Everything you say tends to become manifest. When you say you can do something or you can't, you begin to make the statement come to pass.

Watch your language.

∾

Behind Every Behavior Is a Belief

Whenever you are confused about why you did something, look for a belief.

Beliefs compel you to do what you might otherwise think is stupid. The belief isn't stupid. It's just a belief. Change the belief and you change the behavior.

Most people will have no clue that their behavior comes from their own beliefs. They will want to blame others—the president, the economy, their family, friends, childhood, and so on. Blame is easy. It avoids responsibility.

Recognizing that all behavior is caused by a belief will help you select better beliefs for yourself.

It will also help you understand others.

∾

Reclaim Your Self-Esteem: Transform Your Self-Talk from Negative to Positive
Dr. Joe Rubino

As humans, we are all magnificent by nature. We possess the ability to overcome obstacles, achieve meaningful accomplishments, honor our most important values, attain happiness and contribute our special, unique gifts to others. In short, we can take responsibility for making our lives work optimally. Unfortunately, through the course of experiencing life's challenges, we often lose sight of these facts. From birth and continuing throughout our lifetimes, we encounter countless experiences that can either enhance our self-esteem or erode it. The process of diminishing our self-esteem begins with a simple observation that we somehow do not measure up. We judge ourselves as different and deficient in some way. We decide that we don't belong. From this point, our lives unfold in accordance with our expectations. These expectations directly relate to how we feel about ourselves. Either we are worthy of all the good things life can offer or we deserve pain and suffering because we lack value.

When we judge ourselves harshly, we dramatically diminish our ability to merit love and achieve the success and abundance the world reserves for those most valuable. When we base our actions upon the belief that we lack what it takes to deserve rich relationships, material wealth, and happiness, we trigger those very things we fear most: As our self-esteem insidiously continues to diminish, we find ourselves incapable of directing our lives and fortunes productively. Resignation sets in like dry rot, killing our spirits. This ensures that seeing ourselves as undeserving will viciously cycle into results consistent with this expectation and reinforces our sense of worthlessness. The more our self-esteem drops, the less likely we are to act in a way that will generate positive feedback to elevate our deteriorating self-worth.

The key to reversing the process of self-doubt lies in creating empowering interpretations about things that others say or do rather than negative interpretations that berate us and fuel feelings of inadequacy. Become proficient at distinguishing facts from interpretations.

We, too often, confuse what was actually said or done with the personal meaning we attribute to these occurrences. Those who suffer low self-esteem share a greater tendency to tack negative meanings onto life's events. The significance they place on these situations has negative personal connotations, even when none were intended or existed. These damaging interpretations immediately trigger anger, sadness or fear. These emotions rapidly become familiar and induce a false sense of security. Although we hate feeling angry, sad, or afraid, we continually create explanations of events that land us in these moods. We continually collapse facts with interpretations. The stronger the emotions become, the greater our tendency to attribute incorrect connotations to situations. The more we do so, the further our self-esteem erodes.

The good news is that anyone can learn new behavior of attaching positive or neutral meaning to things that are said or done, replacing the typical negative implications. The first step requires developing the ability to distinguish *facts* from the *interpretations* we attribute to the facts. This is especially useful during times of stress and upset, when the emotions of anger, sadness, or fear are present. Like red flags, these emotions warn us that we are confusing facts with interpretations, triggering the negative self-talk that eats away at our self-esteem.

Let's examine this destructive self-talk in detail. Picture your negative self-talk as a cynical character that clings to your shoulder that we'll call Chip. It's important to distinguish Chip's disparaging voice as an entity separate from and outside yourself. Chip can be male or female and will often take on the persona or qualities of a disapproving parent or early detractor. It is important to distinguish between Chip's pessimistic counsel and the wise guidance of your intuition and conscience. The former is skeptical and fear based whereas the latter reflects wisdom and inner insights. Your intuition is never wrong. It is the knowing inner light that guides you through life's turbulent seas.

In contrast, Chip may be single-minded but not very valuable in championing your excellence or making you feel good about yourself. His job is either to keep you unimportant and protected from risk or on the treadmill forever trying to do better and become worthy. He does this best by whispering nonsense into your ear that causes you to feel bad about who you are. This results in two common scenarios. The first has you sell out your needs and dreams, avoid new situations, and shrink away from your true magnificence. The second has you driven to achieve and prove Chip wrong about how unworthy you are. Maybe you recognize having played out both scenarios in different parts of your life.

Let's examine the first situation. Chip likes it when you become a victim because this makes his job easier. Victims don't belong. People don't like them and they don't look good. Victims also don't risk outside their comfort zones or aspire to any great (and dangerous) accomplishments. They live in a world marked by resignation, a world that excludes them as not good enough to play.

Chip can have you mistakenly believe that it is safer to hide out, quit trying and give up than it is to reach for the stars or go for the gold. He'll have you believing that it's actually better to play it safe, avoid risk and circumvent failure. He is quick to point out all the reasons why you should feel bad about who you are. He prefers that

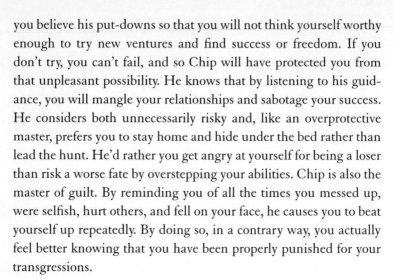

you believe his put-downs so that you will not think yourself worthy enough to try new ventures and find success or freedom. If you don't try, you can't fail, and so Chip will have protected you from that unpleasant possibility. He knows that by listening to his guidance, you will mangle your relationships and sabotage your success. He considers both unnecessarily risky and, like an overprotective master, prefers you to stay home and hide under the bed rather than lead the hunt. He'd rather you get angry at yourself for being a loser than risk a worse fate by overstepping your abilities. Chip is also the master of guilt. By reminding you of all the times you messed up, were selfish, hurt others, and fell on your face, he causes you to beat yourself up repeatedly. By doing so, in a contrary way, you actually feel better knowing that you have been properly punished for your transgressions.

Chip may tell you that life is not so bad if lived quietly, without the stress that accompanies the need to accomplish great things. Maybe you rationalize that you are not experiencing all the bad extremes by playing small and beneath your potential, but perhaps, your life is dimmed, void of the passion and power that would be possible to experience if you played at a higher level. Restoring a healthy sense of self-respect will support you to reclaim your magnificence and generate a variety of new possibilities for happiness and accomplishment.

Chip also can run your life by convincing you that you can overcome your unworthiness if only you try harder and strive for perfection. He has you convinced that your worthlessness can be managed or camouflaged if you climb to the top of that ladder that's leaning against the wall of flawlessness, with the end of the ladder obscured in the clouds above. Once you reach what you think is the top of the ladder, you discover that you're still not perfect, haven't accomplished nearly enough to counter your worthlessness, and must continue to climb the ladder until you reach that faultless state. Of course, the ladder never ends. Perfection is always disappointingly out of reach and mistily out of sight and you get to continually beat yourself up as your life is driven to achieve an unreachable objective. The more Chip berates you as not good enough, the harder you try to be worthy, which you equate with being perfect. Coming from this disempowered state of self-flagellation, you are less likely to be your best and achieve to your potential. There is no peace in this setup.

In either scenario, Chip succeeds in shattering your self-esteem and having you resign yourself to never being good enough by messing with your ability to separate what happened from your interpretations. Reclaiming your self-esteem will result from your ability to recognize when Chip is speaking his nonsense and realize that his misguided counsel does not support your excellence, happiness or magnificence. Guilt is always optional. Instead of berating yourself for your faults, your excellence will result from being able to respond in a manner consistent with your vision, values, commitments, and life purpose.

Also, many of the derogatory messages that Chip whispers did not start with us. We didn't always program the disparaging phrases or misinterpret words or actions, causing our self-esteem to suffer. Many times we were actually told that we were not good enough, unlovable, or unworthy of the best things in life by others. However, we *did* accept and absorb someone else's belittling delusions. Perhaps, a parent, grandparent, or other person told you that you were flawed in some way, and you believed them. Chip now may take on this person's words to remind you of your inferiority. Whether your derogatory thoughts originated from your own misinterpretations or from the unkind words of others, you still have the ability to recognize that these thoughts are untrue and do not support your happiness. You possess the awesome power to stifle your critic every time he or she speaks those critical words.

Chip will never go away for as long as you live. He lives to create dissatisfaction regarding who you are at the core and what your life is about. The more upset, strife, and suffering he helps create, the worse you feel about yourself, and the more Chip is validated. You will find Chip to be especially vocal during times of stress or upset. He uses these opportunities to remind you of how poorly you measure up. The best you can do is to recognize his misguided intention to either protect you from harm or motivate you to be better—and then put in emotional earplugs so you can't hear his sabotaging messages. Recognize his voice when he shows up to speak his opinions and know that you need not listen to what he says. His imprudent, distrustful advice puts you down, ruins relationships, and promotes upset. The most effective way to *temporarily* silence Chip is to forcefully tell him to shut up and take a hike! You need to be as forceful in silencing his cynical chatter as he is in continually dishing it out. Your ability to discern between Chip's dominant disparaging voice and the softer wise counsel of your inner intuition will support your self-esteem to prosper.

Exercise: *For the next week, as you go about your day, notice each time Chip puts you down, makes you wrong, and keeps you small. Record each negative thought you have about yourself. Clearly differentiate Chip's voice from the voice of your trusted intuition. Note how each cynical thought serves some purpose from Chip's perspective. Perhaps it makes you right about something, allows you to dominate others or protects you from potential harm or letdown. Maybe it has you driven to succeed, has you berate yourself with guilt or pity, or has you avoid seizing responsibility for your magnificence. Half the battle in silencing Chip is to recognize when he is speaking to you and realize that his counsel is nonsense. Tell Chip off in a forceful way every time you hear his misguided voice. Replace his negative whispers with positive affirmations that stress your inherent self-worth and value as a magnificent human being.*

Dr. Joe Rubino is a life-changing success coach and an internationally acclaimed business consultant, speaker, and best-selling author of eight books and two tape sets. He is the CEO of The Center for Personal Reinvention, www.CenterForPersonalReinvention.com, an organization committed to the personal excellence and empowerment of all people. His vision is to personally impact the lives of twenty million people to be their best and to shift the paradigm around resignation—that is, that anyone can bring about positive change in their own lives and in the lives of others—if they believe they can. For information on personal coaching and courses, to request his free newsletter, or to learn more about his books and audio programs, visit his web site or contact him at DrJRubino@email.com.

Three Secrets to Manage Your Time

The secret to getting things done is time management.

The secret to time management is to list your to-dos and then prioritize them.

Do first things first.

But here's a secret few know: Your mind can work on some of your to-dos while you do other ones.

In other words, make a list of things you need to do today. Work on the ones that are the most urgent. While you do, allow your unconscious mind to work on other ones.

For example, when I need to write something, such as an article or book chapter, I often ask my unconscious mind to work on it first. This may seem ethereal, but it's a truth in psychology. Turn over as many tasks as possible to your unconscious.

But there's even a deeper secret to time management:

The universe (all that is in the world) will do some of your to-do list for you, if you let it.

When I make a to-do list, I have things in the right column that I plan to do, but I have things in the left column I want the universe to do.

For example, I will make phone calls, write articles, pay bills, run errands. However, I may also request the universe to find the right buyer for a house or to bring me the right contact for my new project, and so forth.

This is truly life's greatest missing secret: The universe will help you get things done if you let it.

❧

Naps Are Good

When the world seems bleak, when you feel out of sorts, when your body feels tired and your mind seems wild, sometimes all you need is a good nap.

❧

Letting Go of Your Fears
Cindy Cashman

Sometimes fear can be paralyzing. Maybe it has stopped you from asking someone new out on a date. For other people fear may have hindered them in making the decision for going after a promotion. Whatever it is, it's important to realize that keeping a healthy *perspective* on what you want is key when handling your fears.

In order to help you create and maintain a clear perspective, I've come up with three additional keys: *Ask*, *Answer*, and *Action*.

Ask

Let's say you want to lose weight. You've tried all the diets, pills, and low fat foods. Still, you're overweight and discouraged. So ask yourself "What is stopping me from losing weight?" Now I have to tell you, this requires total honesty with yourself. This is because you have to really get out of your comfort zone to gain a true perspective on what is blocking you.

Here is an example of how powerful a question can be.

When I was a single mom and had very little money, I asked myself, *"What is stopping me from getting what I want?"* At the time, what I wanted was to make lots of money. That one question completely changed my life for the better.

In my mini power book *The Million Dollar Question Handbook*, I go into more detail about asking quality questions.

If you ask questions such as "Why does this always happen to me?" or "Why are other people luckier than I am?" your life will answer and reflect those answers to you by demonstrating more lack, more bad breaks and more misfortune.

But if you ask questions such as "What is stopping me from using my talents and abilities to create wealth, good health, and joy?" then you give yourself an opportunity to explore the blocks that are keeping you from experiencing the life you want to live. Also ask yourself this question: "What is it that keeps me from going outside my comfort zone?" Thus, you become aware of what is stopping you and can move past it.

Answer

Once you've asked yourself that question, *Answer* it *as honestly as you can*. Really face yourself and search for the answers because this can change your life!

Remember, it only takes one excuse to keep you from losing weight, making a lot of money, or finding that special someone.

Take Action

Action actually consists of two steps: *adopt* and *allow*. In order to take the necessary action, you need to adopt a new perspective and allow yourself to receive the abundance. If either part is left out, you are not likely to complete the necessary action.

Adopt

You see, I believe that deep down, each of us knows what is stopping us from getting exactly what it is we want. And here's the good news: when you realize what it is, you can begin to change your *perspective!* *Adopt* the new perspective, releasing the old one and thereby giving you the freedom to move forward into your new life.

Allow

Now *Allow* yourself to receive the abundance that is yours. Yes, *allow* yourself, because at this point, you should understand that it is only *you* that is preventing you from achieving everything you want to achieve.

A Personal Story of Overcoming Fear One day I had finally had it! I was exhausted from living day to day and just barely getting by. I was determined to figure out a way to break through my financial challenges.

> **The moment I decided that I was fed up with being temporarily out of money was a big changing point in my life.**

So I sat down and promised myself I would take whatever time was necessary to find some answers to my question: "What is stopping me from making lots of money?" I took a piece of paper and made two columns.

At the top of the first column, I wrote: "What is stopping me from becoming rich?" At the top of the second column, I wrote: "What do I need to do to overcome those fears?"

ASK: What is stopping me from becoming rich?	**ASK: What do I need to do to overcome those fears?**

Instantly, the answer came. Without hesitation, a pure knowing filled my being and I *knew* exactly what was stopping me. What is important for you to understand is that any time you ask a question, your mind will search for the answer. It's like a search engine on the internet.

When you use a search engine and type out certain key words or phrases, it will bring up lists that match your requests. Your mind works the same way. That's why you must be careful what kinds of questions you ask. Ask a quality question and you *will* get a quality answer.

The answer that came to me was that a certain friend (we'll call him Bob) was keeping me from becoming financially rich. For an extended period of time, he would call me asking if he could come live with me for a while and if he could borrow money.

Being a single mom without any extra money to lend him, I didn't want to feel responsible for *his* problems, but then I also didn't want to feel guilty because I wasn't being a good friend by not helping him with his problems.

While experiencing those feelings, I wondered about all the problems I might have if I were wealthy. Would I allow him to come live with me? Would I have to help him out all the time? Then I finally realized the reason I was sabotaging my success was that *I did not want to feel obligated to do anything that I did not want to do.*

I realized I had to start being honest to myself. This was a huge turning point for me because I didn't realize how much I was denying. I kept making the excuse that the effects of his actions on me weren't that bad. That kind of excuse can shut down the flow of answers and information you need to eliminate blocks and barriers.

So the left-hand column read "Bob." In the right-hand column it became obvious to me that I needed to learn how to say no—so I did. I was also able to realize that Bob was responsible for his *own* problems.

Once I became totally fed up with my financial situation, asked better questions, and decided to let go of my denial, then I was free to break through my fears and succeed in a massive way.

So here is what it looked like:

Ask, Answer, Adopt and Allow

ASK: What is stopping me from making lots of money?	ASK: What can I do to overcome it?
ANSWER: Bob	ANSWER: Tell him "no."
	ADOPT: I am not responsible for his problems.
	ALLOW: Myself to move forward and have success.

You will come to realize that you are the source of all of your conditions and situations in your life. I thought Bob was the one stopping me from becoming rich, but what I learned was that I had to learn how to handle potential problems upfront and that no one would have that kind of power over me. This is a very powerful process that helped free me.

Now it's your turn. Take out another sheet of paper and begin this process of changing and creating your new perception! Here are some questions to help you get started:

What is stopping me from:

- losing weight?
- getting financially rich?
- having a great relationship?
- starting my own business?
- having the career I want?
- moving forward with my dreams?
- believing in myself?

Next, ask yourself "What do I need to do to overcome it?"

Let the answer come, adopt your new perspective, and allow yourself to achieve and succeed.

———

The above information is from Cindy Cashman and is part of her www.creatingandbuildingwealth.com program.

———

How to Break Through the Hidden Obstacle Holding You Back from What You Truly Want
Craig Perrine

What do you want right now in your life that you don't have? More love? More money? Success and adoration? Better health?

I have a simple exercise that will help to reveal the hidden obstacle that is holding you back.

Ready? Get a piece of paper and take a minute to write down one specific thing that you really want.

Then, write down everything that comes to mind that is standing in your way of getting this one thing that you want. It's really important that you get perfectly clear on what you'll need to break through to get what you want, so make sure you take at least a few minutes to do this before reading on.

Done? Okay, now what's on your list? Is your job lousy? Do you live in the wrong part of town or don't know the right people? Don't have any capital to start the business you've dreamed of? Don't have enough time to learn new skills or take on a new project? At one point, I was plagued by all those handicaps, and more.

Perhaps you face the same obstacles. In fact, it's commonly accepted that those things hold almost everybody from succeeding at one point or another.

Now, complete the exercise by writing "None of these things is truly keeping me from getting what I want."

See, after years of studying some very wise mentors and reading countless books, I learned a secret that helped me overcome those challenges and many, many others, too.

If you think about it, just about anything you've ever truly wanted has required you to overcome some obstacle to get it. So you can imagine how powerful it is to discover this secret and be able to break through any obstacle and attain your desires.

Here's the secret that the wise mentors shared with me (and I admit that it took me years to actually accept it):

> **The only thing holding you back from getting whatever you desire is yourself.**

All those things you wrote down that are in your way are just symptoms of the true obstacle . . . that you believe those things can block you and hold you back.

What you believe is directly related to what you soaked up automatically from the people and events around you from the day you were born. The sad truth is that most of what is pumped into your head is the opposite of what will lead to living a happy life and, in fact, is probably 99 percent of the reason you don't have what you want today.

You will find that your true self is hidden, buried beneath layers of beliefs that you've collected from others without really challenging them. Your true self is a very powerful being, capable of attracting whatever you desire, often quickly and easily and without the struggle that you may have accepted as being required to achieve anything.

As we grow up we are taught to mature and leave behind our fantasies and belief in the magic around us in the world. We worship science and facts and a what-we-see-is-reality view of the world because that is what everyone else believes.

However, there is real magic in the world, and there are books—like Dr. Joe Vitale's best selling *Attractor Factor*—that can show you how to tap into it and draw out what you desire in life.

When I first heard that I was responsible for everything in my life, I initially accepted that and began to beat up on myself for every failure and setback. What was harder for me was to take credit for the powerful results I had created and accept that I could manifest what I wanted at any level imaginable.

Over the years I've learned that being responsible for everything in your life isn't about blame or even boasting for every success, but simply acknowledging the connection between what you do and don't do and how that yields the results you get.

Although you may at first be intimidated and feel reluctant to remove the shield of blaming others and events beyond your control, the truth is that taking full responsibility is the fastest and most powerful way to change what you don't like and add to what you do want in your life.

After all, if something bad happens and you didn't do it, how can you truly fix it? As the creator of your reality, you can take charge and focus your energy on what will get you the results you want and learn to avoid what won't.

Imagine how difficult it would be to learn how to ride a bike if you blamed every spill on the pavement, on the bike, on obstacles that got in your way. Instead, you practice how to balance, how to steer, when to use the brakes, and you learn how to ride a bike.

As they say, you never forget how to ride a bike once you've learned. Well, so it is with taking charge of your life and breaking through obstacles. Once you fully understand how you create your reality, you suddenly have the ability to plot a course to your desires that will truly amaze you because it feels like magic.

If you want to see a movie that is a wonderful metaphor for this principle, watch *The Matrix*. There is a scene in which the main character, Neo, realizes that he has the power to do anything and, in fact, does what he and everyone else formerly believed to be impossible. I won't spoil the movie if you haven't seen it already, but you'll know the moment when you see it.

Whenever I feel overwhelmed and forget what I know about creating my own reality, if I visualize Neo discovering his true unlimited power, I remember.

I'm writing this because too often in life we hear success principles like these: "You are what you believe" and "If you say you can, you can, and if you say you can't, you can't." We become numb to the full meaning these principles hold for us.

It's too easy to let conventional wisdom pack our minds full of comforting nonsense that popular culture feeds us and to overlook the richer, infinitely more powerful truth that we are only limited by our self-imposed boundaries; it is our responsibility to believe what brings us what we want. Movies like *What The Bleep* will open your eyes to exactly how much you truly are in the driver's seat of your life.

So, just as learning to ride a bike seems confusing and even painful at first, once you realize you are doing the steering, you'll be able to finally propel yourself in the direction you want to go in life and ride around any obstacles that appear on your journey.

Craig Perrine is an Internet marketing expert and mentor. See www.easymiracles.com.

❧

Who You See Is Who You Will Be . . .
Kevin Hogan

If there were seven things I would tell my kids to do to be truly successful and achieve in life, one of them would be to select the people they spend time with carefully.

Scientific research clearly reveals that parenting and genetics are important, but they don't hold a candle in influencing behavior (results) that the people in the environment do.

Let me state this is no uncertain terms: If you hang out with losers, you will gravitate toward losing. If you hang out with winners, the same is true. The reason this is the case is simple: We all do things to cooperate or compete with people in our environment. That can be the culture and society on one level or it can be your peer group or neighbors on the other.

Defining a winner and a loser can be difficult. Not everyone you care about is going to be as achievement-oriented as you are. Achievement is a behavior, it is a result. It is what happens when you do specific things that other achievers do.

For me, winners don't have to be wealthy, but they certainly can be. It's one attribute that reveals self-discipline.

Another attribute to look for in others is that of kindness. In this quality, I don't bend much. I don't hang out with unkind people. Unkindness is like a disease. Nice is worth a lot short term and long term, and it is the only way to be.

People who get things done are a must in my environment. I'm not interested in seeing someone start lots of projects. I'm interested in seeing someone finish lots of projects. This, too, is contagious. People who are seeing their work through to completion are exhibiting self-discipline that most people do not have. I will bend on this characteristic but how much time can I invest in people who don't finish projects? Not much.

Because there are no perfect people (and those that appear perfect have plenty of skeletons, I promise you), you want to choose people who are making the attempt. Do **not** pay attention to people who are talking success. Talk is cheap, and all the positive thinking on the planet doesn't get you results; if the positive thinking isn't getting results, it's creating a big problem for you. If you are around the positive talker, you have no better benefit than being around the negative thinker. At least the pessimist is finding the problems that need to be solved.

Meanwhile, if the positive person **is** changing lives, is achieving his or her dreams, *then* you have found someone to put into your master-mind or support team alliance.

Who else do you want to surround yourself with? You want to surround yourself with a true psychic. Someone who sees problems coming, has solutions in advance of the arrival, and is ready to implement them when they arrive and can move on. This person is one of the most valuable people on your team, and developing these characteristics will help you go far, as well.

Finally, you want to choose someone who communicates in real terms. There is no lottery to be won. God is not a slot machine. Almost everything you ultimately achieve in life is going to be because you caused it to happen.

Yes, you can get an inheritance. (I never did, by the way.) You can be raised in a middle or upper income family. (I was raised in a family in the lowest decile of income.) You can be given a big job by a big company because Mom or Dad knew the right person, but over time your legacy, your work, your passion is what gets you to where you are going.

You can't stop the World Trade Center from falling with a prayer, nor can you pray the dying person back to health, but you can cause wonderful event after event to take place in your life and in the lives of those around you. You don't create your entire reality, but you do shape everything that you see in front of you. You created your kids (the neighbor's kids gave them most of their good or bad traits though). Most people created their bank accounts, and those who have had bad things happen in life can be in the process of creating a new bank account.

Everything that is, was first a thought. Buddha said that, not me. I use that as a law or truth in life. Like Edison or Ford, when I think of something, I cause it to happen, and I create the belief that it is my ability to do so regularly, by making sure that my thoughts become reality as often as they need to do so.

Don't hang out with dreamers. Hang out with doers. Do you believe in God? Let's say you do. In the beginning God, dreamed about making the heavens and the earth but got so busy and never got around to it . . . Do you want to hang out with that guy or this guy: In the beginning God created the heavens and the earth . . . and saw it was good.

That's my kind of guy. I'm not saying God is there. That's for you to decide. I do know that you want to be in the presence of people who *do*. People who *do*, *have*. They are the cause, and they are the people that will help you shape your destiny.

Choose well. It makes *all* the difference in your world.

———

Kevin Hogan is the author of several bestselling books, including *The Psychology of Persuasion*.

∽

To Everything, Turn! Turn! Turn!
Alan R. Bechtold

I grew up in the 1960s, and I used to love that wonderful Pete Seeger song, "Turn! Turn! Turn! (To Everything There Is A Season)," as it was recorded by the rock group The Byrds.

However, I am constantly amazed at how many years had passed before the true meaning of that song actually sank in. It's such an important message, I wish I'd seen it earlier. Sadly, only the passing of many years made the meaning crystal clear.

Until I finally saw it, I was a victim of life, pulled along by circumstances, doomed to live the path that lay before me, however twisted or riddled with sharp stones it might have been.

When something bad happened—if my car broke down or I lost a job or even if I threw a party that didn't pan out—I would feel that life had it in for me and there was little I could do to change the path I was on.

Now that I fully understand the significance of Seeger's message, I've been liberated. I now enjoy everything that happens to me—good and bad. I constantly gain experience and knowledge and wisdom from all of life's experiences.

Here's the message, woven not so subtly within Seeger's brilliant, beautiful lyrics, a message that all too often remains elusive, until you've lived sufficient years to discover its real meaning: everything happens for a reason.

There is a plan, much bigger than any of us can see. And everything that life delivers to us fits that plan, is part and parcel of the overall big picture that will forever remain outside our grasp. Nothing happens accidentally and everything that happens is, somehow, intricately connected to a much larger picture.

Knowing this, seeing this, makes all of life's experiences—tragic or ecstatic—take on an entirely new meaning. It also changes your approach when faced with life's challenges.

Knowing the true meaning of those lyrics, understanding the underlying message, I now head into each and every day charged up and fully ready for *any* challenge, big or small, because I know in my heart even the most monumental of setbacks are part of a script, a story line, that inevitably leads to learning, wisdom, and advancement in life.

The most tragic of events are, then, merely stepping stones to greater things. Tests you must not only endure but turn into a benefit, if you are to grow and fit into the unseen plan that is spread out before all of us.

You can't fight the plan, but you can fit yourself *into* it by learning from your mistakes, taking whatever lessons you can find from everything good or bad that happens in your life.

And, believe me, there are *plenty* of lessons to be learned!

So it's not just willy-nilly happenstance, after all. Everything you experience holds the key, somehow, some way, to greater understanding of your place in the plan and your ability to fit into that plan and make it work to better your life.

You are *not* at the mercy of life. You are at the mercy of your own willingness to accept life—*all* of it—and learn everything you can from all that life has to offer you.

You've heard the saying that, without bad, there would be no good. Without bad experiences, you could not appreciate the good experiences that happen.

And here's the most vital key: How you handle the bad things that happen—the way in which you deal with them and learn from them—actually enhances and increases the number and duration of the good things that happen!

I don't claim to understand the overall grand plan. No one can. It is forever beyond our grasp, as it should be. However, we *can* understand the tiny pieces of the puzzle that we are dealt and make the effort to fit those pieces into the larger puzzle so that we fit into the plan and benefit from the enormous bounty of treasures it has to offer all of us who do our part to make the pieces of the puzzle fit.

Bucking the plan, failing to understand life's lessons and joys, is what makes you a victim of life. Flowing *with* the plan, learning from the hardest of experiences life has to offer and growing as a result, makes you fit in, brings you into the fold, and makes life start working for you in ways you could never have imagined.

When I first started publishing online, in 1984, there were these things called computer bulletin boards. I was convinced they were the wave of the future, and I built my entire business around them.

It turns out I was only partially right. Online communications *was* the wave of the future, but I failed to see that computer bulletin boards were *not* the way that future was destined to be realized. They were, instead, merely a stepping stone to the next phase of development for the industry and for me.

I failed to see this until my business nearly failed, as I bucked the change to the World Wide Web. Finally, in 1996, faced with more than $40,000 in personal debt and a company that was tanking quickly, I saw the light and learned my lesson.

Only then did I decide to go with the flow, rather than fight it. I stopped bucking the change and found a way to make my company fit into the change.

The result: I switched gears completely, embraced the Web, and applied my knowledge of online marketing and publishing to this new phase of online communications. Over the next five years, I generated more than $12 million in sales as a direct result!

None of that would have happened had it not been for my first experiences with the early dial-up computer bulletin boards. It was my experience there that led me to a partner who then made it possible, when I finally switched gears and entered the World Wide Web, to make all those sales. I would never have met him had it not been for my earlier failure! That failure led to unimaginable success!

If you realize what I realized too late, you'll be ahead of the game of life from the starting gate. Never fear failure, for even failure holds keys to your next success. Don't hold back because you're afraid you'll make a mistake. Even big mistakes, when they are studied and the lessons learned are properly applied, provide bridges to accomplishments down the road.

Don't forget to also study your successes. Don't ever take success for granted. I experienced a great deal of success with the computer bulletin boards early on.

Sometimes, early success is only a set-up for a failure you must learn from later to truly succeed. Within any success there are clues that can help you repeat the success and build upon it, and there are keys to overcoming the failures that are sure to come later.

Learn this now. See life for what it is. Realize you have control only over your tiny piece of the overall puzzle. Realize that, when you fit your tiny piece into the overall plan, it is there for the good of all.

Then, you will find peace and satisfaction in all life has to offer.

———

Alan Bechtold operates the BBS Press Service. See www.sysop.com.

Ultimately, there are only two answers to EVERY question. Positive and Negative. It's your decision which one to choose.
—NERISSA ODEN, www.TheVideoQueen.com

What I Wish I'd Learned When I Was Younger
Bob Scheinfeld

When I was 12 years old, my grandfather started me on the road to understanding that there are visible and invisible forces shaping what happens to us every day, and that the invisible forces are where the real power is.

The revolutionary information my grandfather shared with me took me to many places in my pursuit of knowledge and inspiration: traditional science, esoteric teachings, metaphysics, new age thought, quantum physics, and so forth.

As I studied and worked, three core questions surfaced that I felt compelled to answer:

1. Who am I?
2. Why am I here?
3. What is my purpose?

I had no problem answering question number one. To me, we're all amazing beings whose natural state is infinite power, wisdom, and abundance. That is, we're all Godlike at our core.

I had no problem answering question number two either. To me, we all come to the human experience to play and have adventures, just as we go to movies and amusement parks.

I also had no problem answering question number three. To me, our purpose is simply to explore and have the experiences we came here to have.

As I probed more deeply into life's mysteries, however, especially after having some mind-blowing experiences and studying recent developments in quantum physics, another core question came to mind:

Is the human experience and all we see around us real?

When I say *real*, I mean is it solid and tangible? Does it have any existence independent of us? Does it have any real power in and of itself? Such questions may seem unnecessarily theoretical, but the answers actually have tremendous practical value in our lives.

What I concluded, what many esoteric teachings suggested and recent developments in quantum physics document (but what neither fleshes out in a practical way), and what I wish I'd learned when I was younger, is that the human experience, the whole physical universe we all play in, is *not* real.

It's all an illusion, a hologram, or what I call a total immersion movie experience, created by the combination of consciousness and tremendous power, which makes it appear real. Life is all a game being played *in* consciousness and it's our power, as the infinite beings we are, that fuels it.

What I wish I knew earlier is that, if you can really understand that, and make several important shifts in your own consciousness, you can tap into sources of unimaginable power to redesign and reshape literally everything you experience in your life.

It's kind of like having what is called a lucid dream in which you wake up in the middle of the dream and take total control over everything happening within it. I would have loved to have awakened within my human experience a lot earlier than I did!

———

Bob Scheinfeld is the best-selling author of *The Invisible Path to Success* and *The 11th Element*. For more than 20 years, he has helped individuals in more than 170 countries create extraordinary results, in less time, with less effort, and much more fun. For more information, visit: http://www.7powercentersoflife.com.

∾

The Great Philosophers Were Only Giving You Their Views

All the great philosophers and psychologists you've ever heard of are all giving you their opinion. They have a map of how they think the world works. That map is their philosophy or psychology. It isn't necessarily true. It's their opinion.

You can create your own view of the world. You can choose an existing philosophy or psychology or even make one up. Few people know that we all have the choice.

EXTERNAL CONNECTIONS

*Caring for Others
in Your Life*

The Most Valuable Life Lesson You'll Ever Learn
Chip Tarver

Here it is. Remember and use this one even if you forget everything else you've ever learned or been taught:

The Golden Rule—Treat others as you want to be treated, or treat them as they want to be treated.

That's a million-dollar primary principle. Literally.

There is no other better precedent around which to fashion your life than this guiding primary principle. When you put yourself aside and consider others first, people not only remember you—they want to be around you.

Why?

Using this principle means you're a great listener. Too many people are too interested in what they have to say to be quiet enough long enough to hear what you have to say.

Too many people are too concerned with their own needs and wants, so they don't take time to consider yours. We see these important issues affecting marriages and jobs every day.

When you separate yourself from the pack by putting other people first, being a great and active listener, and then respond with the primary idea of creating a win-win situation for everyone involved—you're a winner. Take that to the bank, literally.

When you try to help people get what they want, the Law of Reciprocation says that they'll want to help you get what you want. That's not being selfish, it's simply being wise. You just set into motion a spiritual law that no one can stop.

This is a primary principle of life that not only blesses all the people around you; it also directly translates into great relationships and more deposit tickets at your bank.

So never forget: Always give first, and always be sure to employ the most important life principle—The Golden Rule—today and every day. It's a system that's proven to work. Every time.

❧

Your Relationships Are for Your Growth

Don't expect any long-term relationship to be smooth sailing. The bumps, hills, and valleys, rises and falls are life's way of helping you grow. If you give up and bow out, you may miss a great lesson (and you'll end up in another relationship that will give the lesson to you in a more dramatic way).

The point is to stay together and grow, not separate and sulk. You may come to a moment when you both, calmly and respectfully, decide to move down different paths, but jumping out of a moving car isn't wise or healthy. Stay in your seat and enjoy the ride.

Practice forgiveness, tolerance, and compassion. This won't always be easy, but it will always be for your growth.

❧

Your Parents Did the Best They Could

I never liked how my father raised me. He was an ex-Marine drill sergeant and a former professional boxer. He treated me like a drafted recruit in World War II. I grew up resenting the beatings, the discipline, and the constant terror.

A friend of mine in college shocked me when he said, "Your father could have tossed you in a garbage can when you were a baby. He didn't. He raised you the best way he knew how."

I've since learned that all parents are winging it. None of them went to parenting school. Few of them read parenting books. Most of them raise their kids either the way they were raised or the opposite of the way they were raised. None of them raised their kids with ill intent. They were doing the best they could.

Your parents did the best they knew how to do, based on their beliefs, upbringing, and best guess about how to handle you.

Forgive them. Understand them. Love them. All they want from you at this point is to know that you understand they did the best they could. Tell them so. Don't withhold the very thing they long to hear.

~

Your Children Will Become What They Become

How can you tell if your child will grow up to be the next Dali Lama?

You can't.

My sister has twins. They were raised in the same environment, by the same parents, had the same teachers in the same schools, and dated sisters.

In spite of that, they are completely different in personalities and goals.

Water your children with love and allow them to grow as they choose.

And be sure to give them each a copy of this manual.

~

You Can Achieve Anything with Support

You will find that getting results in your life is easier when you have people supporting you.

I'm not talking about financial support, though you might think that would be nice. Instead, I'm talking about emotional support.

Whether you want to lose weight, quit smoking, increase your income, build a business, raise a family, or most anything else, having a support team will make the process much easier for you.

Most people in life will want to achieve things on their own. Ultimately, whatever you achieve will be because of your own efforts, but having others encourage you will make it easier for you to make the efforts needed for success. It's the difference between running a marathon alone, or running one with a crowd to cheer you on.

This works the other way around, too.

Helping others by encouraging them will help you. You will feel satisfaction from their wins, and you will increase your own energy as you offer some to others.

In short, be willing to ask for and offer help to achieve your dreams.

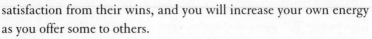

Listening
John Milton Fogg

In the beginning, it is written, was the word. Problem is, nobody was listening. Besides the universal life purpose that I believe all human beings share of learning to love and be loved, *listening* is the life lesson I wished I'd learned long ago—in the beginning.

"Listen," my mentor, Carol McCall said (and so titled her book), "there's a world waiting to be heard." All you need do is read a magazine, newspaper, blog, or (perish the act) turn on the television to learn how people, communities, corporations, countries are not listening—and the tragic price they are paying for not listening.

Even though 85 percent of what we know we learn by listening, researchers have found that we are distracted, preoccupied, or forgetful three-quarters of the time. Oh we *hear* what people are saying, but we're not *listening*. Not really. Proof? More research: We only remember 20 percent of what we hear. Why? Because although we listen to between 125 to 250 words per minute, we think at 1,000 to 3,000 words per minute, and while other people are speaking, we're thinking, thinking, thinking.... Here's what William Stringfellow wrote in the Quaker monthly *Friend's Journal:*

Listening is a rare happening among human beings. You cannot listen to the word another is speaking if you are preoccupied with your appearance, or with impressing the other, or are trying to decide what you are going to say when the other stops talking, or are debating about whether what is being said is true or relevant or agreeable. Such matters have their place, but only after listening to the word as the word is being uttered. Listening is a primitive act of love in which a

person gives himself to another's word, making himself
accessible and vulnerable to that word.

Simple science shows us that no two things can take up the same space at the same time. So it is with *listening.* You cannot think and listen; read and listen; day dream and listen; write and listen; agree, disagree, argue, interpret, mind read, rehearse, plot, plan, placate, or even listen and *listen.* (Apologies to the multitasking gender.) Listening requires our full and focused attention on the other person. Real listening truly honors people. Authentic Listening can actually heal people.

One bit I appreciate most about the quote from Stringfellow is "Listening is a primitive act of love. . . ." What makes that special and important for me is that it takes me right back to the beginning. If, as I said and believe, every human being shares the same life purpose to learn to love and be loved, then *listening* gives me a simple—though not easy to master—truly elegant power tool to fulfill my life's purpose.

Yet the number of us who have had formal educational experience in listening is less than two in every hundred people. I wished I'd learned to listen long, long ago.

———

John Milton Fogg, author, *The Greatest Networker in the World.*

What You Do Influences People Down the Chain

Few people stop to think about the fact that how they treat people is part of a chain that influences all people.

On the level that is simplest to understand, when you smile at someone on the street, that person may be uplifted to such a degree that they smile to the next person they see, who then smiles to the next person *they* see, and so on, down the chain. This single act can uplift a lot of people.

By the same token, when you get angry, or give someone a dirty look, the person who received your negativity may pass it on to the next person they see, who passes it to the next person they see, and so on. It becomes a mind virus.

Control the virus.

Send out positive signals to influence the world chain.

It all begins with you.

~

People Like Nice People

I've met a few celebrities. When I tell people at my seminars or in private about them, they always want to know one thing: "Are they nice?"

We all like people who are nice—meaning pleasant, smiling, approachable, friendly.

This is a clue about how to live your life.

Be nice.

~

People Want to Be Loved

When my father was building a house for his family, the electrician he hired became his best friend. They ate together, made wine together, drank it together, and laughed and told stories. My father listened to anything his new friend told him, because my father wanted the feeling of being loved. He also wanted a sound house, of course, but he was only going to hire the electrician he trusted, which, of course, was the electrician who showed the most love for my dad. Neither man would ever say they felt love for the other, but deep down, just like every one of us, what they longed for was love. Help people feel loved and they will pay you in gold.

~

Having a Role Model Can Bring Out the Best in You

Most people imitate the people around them: family, friends, teachers, or characters on television or from the movies. The problem is, there are limits to what these role models bring out of you. If you truly want to strive for the best, then emulate the best. This *may* mean following the lead of family, friends, or celebrities. It might also mean looking elsewhere.

For example, when I got into body building, I wanted to follow the best. Although there were several famous people to choose from, I selected Steve Reeves, who was the original Hercules in the movies. Although I will never look exactly like Reeves, by modeling myself after him I was able to transform my body from fat to fit.

Others have copied Roy Rogers, the happy singing cowboy, to find the hero within themselves. The point is, throughout life you may find people who will disappoint you. The idea is to find someone who has the traits you want to develop, and model yourself after those traits. You don't want to become the person you are imitating; instead you want to develop the strengths they have within yourself.

Of course, if Superman is your role model, be sure to stay away from kryptonite.

How to End an Argument

Be the first to say, "I'm sorry."

As soon as you say it, the other side will look at you to see if you are sincere. If you are, the tension will release.

How to Deal with an Enemy

Ask them for their advice.

Few people can resist being asked for their advice.

You position yourself as open minded and the enemy will open to you.

The Man Who Offered to Beat Me Up

Today I received a long letter from a man who created a new self-defense system. He claims he can defeat anyone in under three minutes.

He wants me to promote him and his method. He went on to say he'd be happy to meet with me to prove his skills.

What did he have in mind?

He wants to beat me up.

I'm serious.

"If I can defeat you within three minutes," he said in his letter, "then you promise to promote me and my products. Deal?"

He went on to give me the contact information for his agent so I could set up the match.

It might have made an interesting webcast. I can just see the headline:

> **51-year-old, formerly obese, Internet Marketing Expert meets 30-year-old Superman-fit Martial Arts Expert in Quick-Kill Match. Register now.**

Gee, I wonder who would win?

I'd lose even if I went armed.

What would you have done?

How would you have responded to his offer?

Unless you're a fighter looking for a match, you'd probably toss this offer in the trash.

I often wonder what people are thinking. Does this guy really think I'll fight him? And then, if I lose, I'll gladly smile and start marketing him?

I don't claim to be a fighter and am not seeking bouts. I'm also not seeking new clients. Especially clients who want to break my nose to prove they are better than me.

When you reach out to anyone, keep in mind that no one likes to be told they are inferior. It is not a good way to win friends and influence people. In fact, it's not a good way to do much of anything.

I think the lesson here is that we all have egos. The better way to approach people is to put your ego under theirs.

In other words, be willing to lower your status. Don't flaunt your stuff. Instead, show your weakness and ask for help.

This nervy fighter might have done better by offering to teach me his new method, not offering to embarrass me with it.

Take heed.

⁓

Everyone Is Going through Something

You may think you are the only person suffering from money worries, or health issues, or relationship problems, or—just name it.

The truth is, everyone is going through something. Knowing this can help you be more understanding of others. The person who just cut you off on the freeway may have just lost his job, or had a child do something wrong, or may be sick.

Just as you have bad days, and events that you must wrestle with to learn and grow, so do others.

Just as you want them to understand your life, you need to understand theirs.

Mutual understanding can bring peace to the world.

⁓

Failing Life
Bill Harris

I flunked life lessons 101 several times before I figured out why. The area I flunked most often was romantic relationships.

I'm the spitting image of my father and share many of his mannerisms. My mother, who ultimately came to dislike my father, and who divorced him when I was three years old, spent my adolescence telling me, "You're just like your father—no woman will ever put up with you."

Because such deeply held beliefs tend to manifest themselves in reality (something I did not know at the time), I was continually attracted to women who seemed to have been custom-designed to help me prove the truth of what my mother had told me. The drama would play out in one of two ways. I would either attract a woman who, because of her own problems, could not nurture a man, had a lot of trouble being intimate, and who had a lot of anger toward men, or, if I somehow accidentally attracted someone who was emotionally healthy, I would find a way to drive her away with my own emotional problems.

I replayed this scenario at least twenty times during my adult life. I met and fell over and over for essentially the same woman, but each time in a different body. With minor variations, the story had the same plot line and the same tragic ending every time.

Eventually, in an attempt to clear up this and other emotional problems, I learned to meditate. Later I began to meditate with the very powerful Holosync audio technology that I now offer through my company, Centerpointe Research Institute. As I meditated each day over several years, I began to develop a deeper awareness of what I was doing and how I was creating these relationship disasters.

I began to see the entire process in slow motion, from the first blush of attraction to the dance of courtship to the emergence of different but interlocking emotional dysfunctional behaviors of me and my partners, to the eventually acrimonious and unhappy parting. As I was increasingly able to stand aside from what was happening and watch it with a new awareness, two things happened. First, it became more and more difficult to summon up my formerly boundless enthusiasm for the whole exercise. Somehow standing aside and watching the process from a more aware perspective, and knowing in advance how it would turn out, made it increasingly difficult to continue.

Second, I realized that the feeling of intense attraction that I had always assumed meant "Here is a candidate to pursue for a romantic relationship" did not mean that at all. Instead, it actually meant "Here is someone who will help you prove that your mother was right—that no woman will be able to put up with you."

Seeing this in this new way was a soul-searing experience. As a result, I found myself not responding in the same way to this feeling of attraction. Instead, I was able to watch myself have the feeling and, knowing in advance where it would lead and what would happen, to leave it alone.

Ironically, within a very short period of time, my ability to watch this feeling rather than act on it led me to attract a totally different kind of woman, one who was warm and loving and nurturing, and who was not there to play out the same script. Today, I'm happily married to a wonderful woman who deeply loves me.

There were several lessons in this for me, and I really wish I could have learned them 30 years sooner. The first was that what we believe does indeed create the circumstances and realities of our lives. It wasn't true that no woman would ever put up with me, but by strongly believing that it was, I did create it in reality. I have been able to use this wisdom to clear up many other areas of my life that were not working as well as I wanted.

Second, I learned that when any belief is made conscious, and you are able to watch the creative process set in motion by that belief, from the first impulse to the end result, such beliefs dissolve—if they do not serve you. You can continue to create the same negative consequences for decades if you do it unconsciously, but once you begin to do so with awareness, what does not serve you falls away as if by magic.

Third, people have much more control over what they create in life than at first they believe. For many years I continued to create painful relationships, feeling like a victim of circumstances, bad people, and other external events. When I learned, however, that what was happening was my own doing (though unintentional), and was the inevitable result of what I was doing inside my own head, I found that I had all the power and control I needed to shape my life in any way I wanted. As the great Napoleon Hill, author of *Think and Grow Rich* said, "The one and only thing over which each person has total and complete control is how they focus their mind."

Luckily, this seemingly small ability is the key to everything else, and I feel grateful that I finally learned this.

Bill Harris is CEO of www.centerpointe.com.

TROUBLESHOOTING

~

Taking Care
of Yourself

The Universe Always Says Yes

The universe (the energy of all that is in your life) will always say yes to your thoughts.

If you think negative thoughts, the universe will say "Okay, I agree with you," and bring you negative results.

If you think positive thoughts, the universe will say, "Okay, I agree with you," and bring you positive results.

In every situation, the universe will say yes.

Once You Get the Lesson, You Don't Need the Experience

Once you get the lesson of any experience, you don't need to repeat the experience.

Until you get the lesson, you will continue to recreate the experience, escalating in pain, until you get the lesson.

In other words, notice that people seem to keep having the same problem. One person may get married seven times. One person may always struggle with money. Another person may have the same health issue reoccur.

None of these are predestined or set in stone. Get the lesson the experience is offering you and the experience will leave.

Pay attention to your lessons.

Give What You Want to Receive

Everyone will talk you out of this principle, but the truth remains, give more of whatever you want to receive.

If you want money, give money.

If you want love, give love.

The trick is to give without expecting return from any one particular source. Allow the return to surprise you.

Give with a joyous, expectant heart, but with an open mind, too.

❦

You Get the Results You're Supposed to Get

It may be hard to accept, but the results you're getting are the results you're supposed to be getting.

In other words, whatever you are doing right now is bringing you the results you are getting right now.

If you are overweight, you probably did something to get that way. Get dropped off in a desert or a prison camp and you'll probably get thin.

If you're alone, it's probably because you did and are doing things to keep people at bay. Join enough Internet chat sites or go to enough parties or meetings and you'll meet people.

If you're broke, you're probably spending more than you need to be or not doing all you need to in order to bring in the money.

When you look at your life objectively, you can see that the results you are getting are exactly the results you should be expecting.

Change what you are doing and you can change your results.

Pretty simple, really.

❦

This, Too, Will Pass

Whatever you are experiencing right now, good or bad, painful or pleasurable, will pass.

I liked the movie *Eternal Sunshine of the Spotless Mind* because it suggested (at least to me) that we are always running from the moment. Rather than enjoying what is—whatever it may be—we are doing our best to escape to the future or to the past.

When you realize that this (whatever this moment is for you) will pass, it may help you appreciate this moment.

If you like this moment, dwell on it because it will soon be gone.

If you don't like this moment, relax, as it will soon be gone.

Be Not Afraid

One of the recurring statements of most philosophers and religions is that life is not scary. You'll find yourself wanting to stop because of fear. You may want to ask for a date, or a raise, or for a loan, but fear will often stop you.

The big secret is that there is nothing to fear.

This will be hard to accept because of your mind, which will terrify you with scenarios to make you afraid.

Again, be not afraid.

Do the thing you wish, and walk through the fear.

On the other side, is freedom.

What You Fear May Contain What You Seek

You may find that the very thing you seek is hidden within the very thing you fear.

For years I was afraid to reveal my spiritual side to the world. I was the author of numerous books for conservative companies, such as the American Marketing Association, the American Management Association, and Nightingale-Conant. I did not want the world to know that I had a softer, loving side. I feared they would judge me.

When I finally released my books, such as *The Attractor Factor*, largely because I was nudged by friends to share them, the response was overwhelming. The book became an Amazon and Barnes & Noble bestseller. None of my books have been anywhere near as successful as that one.

You may find that the thing you fear sharing with the world may be the very thing the world thirsts for. When you share your fear, you may find it rewards you with what you seek.

~

Be Willing to Delay Gratification to Achieve Astonishing Results

You'll find most people will give in to their whims and urges, without much thought to tomorrow.

You'll also find that you'll feel stronger, happier, and will achieve greater results if you delay gratification in favor of a long-term, larger reward.

For example, the best way to lose weight is to ignore the impulse for unhealthy food and instead focus on the end result: a lean body and a longer life.

I've found it easy to ignore desserts or any food temptation by realizing that consuming it now will give momentary pleasure, something that may only last one minute and that I'll regret for weeks or months or even years.

Instead, if I ignore the impulse and focus on the long-term gain, the decision is easier to make.

~

The Lesson That Takes a Lot of the Speed Bumps Out of Life
Ann Taylor

If given the opportunity to go back and restructure my life with only one change or to learn one lesson, it would be to trust my intuition, gut, or sixth sense. There are many names for this part of me that always has my highest and best interest at heart and that reveals to me instructions and guidance in many forms. My life would have been entirely different if I would have known that a feeling of uneasiness is a signal that more investigation is needed before any action is taken on my part. There are so many times that I've blindly followed what others thought was right, others being authority figures such as parents or teachers who had perfectly logical reasons and data to back up why something needed to be done a certain way. Sometimes they were correct, and sometimes they were way off in their guidance. Like so many people, I gave my power away to the outer authority rather than checking with my inner authority or intuition or, as I choose to call it, God.

I was brought up in a middle class family that valued formal education and had very high expectations, which I swallowed hook, line, and sinker. My sister became a pharmacist and my brother an attorney, with my father paying most of the expenses. My father and I didn't get along, but I gave it my best shot. I worked my way through two years of college before stopping, because my heart wasn't in it. At that time, I didn't know what I wanted to do next, but I did know I didn't want to pursue my degree. I even had someone in my life who was willing to underwrite a considerable portion of the expenses for me to continue. Even though I was grateful, it didn't influence my decision not to continue.

I always believed I could do anything I wanted to and be successful as long as I delivered the goods. This has proven true in my life. I chose to take a class from Merrill Lynch at night when I was nineteen years old because the stock market fascinated me. I fell in love, got married, and moved to Naples, Florida where I became a draftswoman for the Department of Transportation (DOT). I really didn't have any passion for the job. This nudged me to start scanning the classified ads. My former husband found an opening being advertised for two stockbrokers. They wanted people who were at least 40 years of age, with experience. I had a very strong desire to apply for this position, and I wanted it very badly. I had just turned 25 and had no experience but lots of willingness. I can still remember the interview as if it were yesterday. I was offered the job at half the salary I was making, and I was thrilled. The rest is history. I found a career I was passionate about. I lived, ate, and breathed the industry. I became a stockbroker five years later when only 2 percent of the people in the industry were women. I didn't know anything about intuition. I didn't know about this homing device that kept me on track in so many ways. I can remember one of many instances in which I advised a client to purchase a stock because I really had a very good feeling about it after I'd done some research. After he had made a good profit, he sold it. At a later date, he wanted to buy it back. I didn't have a good feeling about it, so I told him he might want to wait. He decided to purchase it anyway. Well, you guessed it. The stock headed south, never to see the price again that it was purchased at.

How many times have you said, "I knew that was going to happen"? How many times have you said, "I knew I shouldn't have done that"? If you're like me, you have a pretty long list. It has taken years and a lot of practice for me to get to trust the guidance that I get from God, above anything else.

I recently had a situation in my life that made me understand that there are people that lie so well and convincingly that they can pass lie detector tests. This is no joke. These people are very charming. The person that I encountered didn't set off any of my usual warning signals. The only way, and I stress the *only* way, I knew that this person was lying was to check within. Because I'm the oldest child, makes me the family hero; it also means that I can be denser than a brick when it comes to "getting it" sometimes. This was certainly one of those times. It also gave me my PhD in trusting my guidance, which I will never ever forget. What I learned from this experience is that my connection to God and the guidance that I get is invaluable. I read a book about pathological liars, *The Sociopath Next Door* by Martha Stout, who'd been studying people like this for over 20 years. The book said that the only way you could not be taken advantage of by people like this was to know them over a long period of time. This seemed like a lot of wasted time and energy to me. A much faster way and one I will always use when I meet anyone from now on is to trust my guidance from God.

When I speak before a group I always say that a rock, to an ant, looks like a mountain and, to a 6-foot man, it looks like a rock, and they're both correct. It's a matter of perspective. When you ask a person his or her opinion, what you're getting is their perspective or spin. Every successful person—and the more successful they are the more they do this—trusts their intuition. There are times when you've done all the investigation and you have all the facts. You have consulted with people you know who can give you guidance and whose advice you trust. You know you've done all you can do to determine a course of action to take, which seems obvious and logical and yet, there's that feeling that this isn't the time or the action that needs to happen. I feel that everyone who reads this will know exactly what I'm talking about. It's been my experience that it is in my best interest to not take the action that seems right but to do what I'm being guided to do, even though it flies in the face of all the evidence to the contrary.

After many challenging years, I finally realized what burn-out meant. I knew I needed to take some time off to reflect on what I wanted and where my life was headed. When I was ready to get back into the business arena, I meditated about what to do. In meditation, I was told to go to work for Silent Unity's prayer room, which is a Unity Church's prayer ministry that's been in operation for over 100 years. They have 3 shifts with approximately 25 people per shift that pray with people who call in. After I received that message from meditation, I said "you want me to do what?" I came out of meditation and thought, wrong voice. Well, I went back into meditation, asked again, and got the same answer. The voice said, "You'll love it more than any job you've ever had, and it won't last long." I asked questions, which were answered, and then my guidance stopped. It said, "Go and apply and you will get the rest of your answers." Well, I didn't do what I was told to do. My guidance dogged my heels, which it very seldom does. It kept saying, "You haven't gone to Silent Unity yet." Well, I finally did and was accepted. I started at $7.10 per hour, answering the phone and saying, "Silent Unity, how may we pray with you?" I absolutely loved that job. To me it wasn't a job. Eight months after I started, Unity posted a notice for a development officer. My guidance said, "Apply for this position," which I did. When I had my final interview with Chris Jackson, the senior VP, he said, "Ann, did anyone look at your resume when you applied to the prayer room?" I said, "Chris, I was told by my guidance to go there and now my guidance told me to apply for this job." You guessed it. I got the position. It is through this position that my present career, which is a calling for me, came about. I have an energy-healing and business-coaching practice that spans the globe. I absolutely have the most fun when I'm working with this

awesome gift. I'm humbled by the magnitude to which God has touched my life and the lives of others through me.

You can learn to trust your guidance by practicing. The very best way I know how to learn is through meditation. Most people don't do this because they can't seem to shut off the mind chatter. I studied transcendental meditation about 25 years ago. It was fabulous. I'm now in the process of creating a CD that will greatly reduce or eliminate the mind chatter altogether and relax your body in about five minutes. By the time you read this, it will be on the market. When my mind is quiet and I'm at peace and not attached to results, I get the very clearest guidance. I have to let go of what I feel the guidance should be. Years ago, it felt like I was making up the answers, and it still feels like that. The difference is that with practice, I've come to trust it. I learned to be clear about what I'm asking, so when it's really important to me, I write it down and revise what I've written until it's really clear. I wouldn't give up this ability for Bill Gates's net worth. Where would I be without it? I'd feel like a rudderless ship.

When I'm doing work with clients, often they have issues in mind they want to deal with, such as no longer wanting life to be a struggle. Their lists usually contains 20 to 25 different items like this. There are many ways sessions with clients go. I totally let go and trust that what is done and the order in which it is done is far better coming from God than anything I could possibly come up with for clients. Many times, as I'm working a client will say, "How did you know to heal that?" Because it was one of their really big issues or the client will say, "You keep hitting the big ones, one after the other" or "That was the next one on my list." I tell them, "You know it the same time that I do, when it crosses my lips." I never trust my guidance so much as when I'm in front of an audience, teaching and healing, or doing the same one-on-one with a client. It comes so naturally to me because I've been doing it for over 10 years now. I work at least two hours every day perfecting the work, and many times they are my favorite two hours of my day.

Trusting my guidance is one of the major ways I've found to eliminate a lot of the speed bumps of life. I was told that the man who founded Lord & Taylor, the famous department store, named it that way because his last name was Taylor and the Lord was his guidance. Well, he thought of it first.

————

Ann Taylor, President, Inner Healing, Inc. www.innerhealing.com.

∾

Miracles Happen All the Time—No Exceptions

Miracles happen all the time.

You'll take them for granted.

The fact that you are here is a miracle.

Miracles are what happen beyond immediate comprehension. Explaining it doesn't dismiss the miracle.

Scientists may describe what makes grass green. Their explanations will seem logical, but all they did was put words together in a way to try to rationalize what they can't understand. The explanation doesn't hide the miracle.

Look for miracles.

∾

Confusion Is the Wonderful State before Clarity

At times in your life you will become confused.

It's okay.

Confusion is that wonderful state right before clarity.

∾

The More Clutter around You, the More Clutter in You

A missing secret is this: the more clutter in your room, the more clutter in your mind.

Clean out your closets. Clean out your garage. Clean out your office. Clean out your rooms.

Energy moves when blocks are removed.

Clutter equals blocks.

Hire someone to clean up your areas, if you need to. Or call 1-800-Got Junk? to come and remove your debris.

❦

The Night Window Is Your Chance to Place Your Order

Few know that when they drift off to sleep, they are merging with the energy of all that is, what some call the Universe. This is your opportunity to place a wish or an order, and the Universe will begin to fulfill it.

So as you lay in bed, make a wish.

Wish for whatever you want, preferably something that makes you smile.

Wish for it for yourself or others.

But wish.

And then drift into sleep, smiling, trusting, knowing that it will come to be.

❦

Welcome Ghosts

I've been haunted by three ghosts in my life. The third one just appeared last month. I never know why they pick me, but the relationship usually leads to a brief glimpse of fame and fortune. Maybe this time won't be any different.

The first ghost came to me in 1989. I was reading the famous *Robert Collier Letter Book* and came across the name Bruce Barton. I'm sure thousands have read the same book, saw the same name, but did not have the same experience I had.

I got chills. Something awakened inside me. I began a two-year quest to learn all I could about this now-forgotten advertising genius and bestselling author.

The result was my book, *The Seven Lost Secrets of Success*. It's been through 11 printings. One person bought 19,500 copies of it and gave them as gifts to everyone in his company. The ghost of Barton led me to write the book. It has touched lives around the world and continues to do so. But Bruce Barton was only the first ghost.

The second ghost was P.T. Barnum. The famous showman and

circus promoter came to me while I was reading his autobiography. That led to my quest to learn his business secrets. A year later, I wrote the book, *There's a Customer Born Every Minute*. It also led to my audio program with Nightingale-Conant, *The Power of Outrageous Marketing*. The program has been a bestseller for over five years now.

The third ghost came to me last month. I have been a fan of Neville, the mystical writer of several books, for a decade or more. I even mention him and quote him in my latest book, *The Attractor Factor*. I even called one of the steps in the book, on manifesting with feeling, "Nevillize." You Nevillize a goal when you feel as if you already have it. However, that apparently wasn't enough for Neville.

A few weeks ago I noticed an article about him in a major magazine. That reawakened my interest in the Barbados mystic. I searched and found some of his audios. These are actual recorded speeches he gave in the 1950s and 1960s. I found a man who owned all known recordings of Neville. I bought all 106 of them. I felt as if Neville was speaking to me as I listened to them.

Then I found five lessons Neville taught in 1948. These are very rare. They are about practical metaphysics and how to manifest your heart's desires. Pure gold. I relished the fact that I was somehow led to the lessons, but something shocking happened as I read them.

Neville was talking about needing to take a ship back to his home country. He said the boat's name was *Nerissa*. That is the second time I've heard that name. It's the name of my beloved partner, who I've been with for six years now. Too weird. But the ghostly events didn't stop there.

In the very same week that I found the rare lessons, someone posted five books by Neville on eBay. All were first editions, perfect condition, and autographed. Neville showing up on eBay is odd enough. For five signed books to appear was even stranger. Of course, I bought them all. The adventure didn't stop there.

A few days later eBay notified me that another Neville item was just put online for bidding. I looked and couldn't believe what I saw. It was the original published lesson plan from the 1948 lectures I had discovered—and the manual was autographed.

Then, a few days after that, yet another Neville item went on eBay. This turned out to be a truly rare book from 1939 called *At*

Your Command. I had never heard of it before. Apparently neither had other Neville fans, who had been quiet until now, as the bidding grew hot. In only one day, people were bidding $500 for this little gem. I, of course, wasn't going to let this one slip by. I bid $1,500 for it and won it for $515.

Is the book worth it? I used it to attract a new car: a BMW 645Ci is being built for me right now in Germany. So if having ghosts in my life isn't weird enough, I paid $515 for a little book that is sharpening my powers to manifest what I desire, which is today a $90,000 luxury sports car.

This is getting too strange. The events were reminding me of my experiences with Bruce Barton and P.T. Barnum. I have no idea if the ghosts of these great men were actually contacting me or not, but you have to admit that the synchronicity of events leading me to write my books has been uncanny. No wonder I've been a fan of Rod Serling, who I met when I was a teenager. I *live The Twilight Zone.*

I'm not sure why Neville is contacting me. Maybe it's just to dust off his message and present it to a new audience (meaning you). Meanwhile, he'll notify me tonight, or tomorrow. I know he would like his ideas made available, so I put some of them online at http://www.AttractANewCar.com

There's a greater lesson here. The joy in life is in following joy. What I mean is, whether paying attention to these coincidences leads to a new book or not isn't as important as the thrill of acting on them. The adventure is in the journey, not in the destination. The destination is simply a pause before the next journey.

Are you acting on the nudges you get, even when you have no idea where they will lead? If so, you will find life exhilarating. And you might even meet a ghost or two.

Do Not Strive for Perfection

The quest for perfection will stop you from getting results throughout your life. Realize right now that *perfection* is a relative term. What seems perfect to you will seem flawed to someone else; what seems perfect to them will seem ridiculous to you. It's all a matter of opinion.

Do the best you can and let go. History will judge what you have done. And more often than not, it will forget and forgive all of us.

Enjoy the journey.

It's perfect as it is.

All is well.

❧

Perfect As Is
John Burton

It took me several decades of living to realize that nothing is perfect in life except everything. Allow me to explain. For many years I suffered from what I call dyslexic logic, getting cause and effect reversed. Actually I've come to realize that there is no such thing as cause, but that's for another time. For a long time I used to think, like so many people do, that I had to behave in a certain way or achieve certain levels of success in order to gain self-worth. I believed that, to stave off some nagging sense of inferiority or imperfection, I simply must make perfect choices and behave in perfect ways. At best, self-worth would be the temporary byproduct of these perfect acts. The chase was on! Of course, the degree of success was frustratingly inconsistent, only feeding the awareness of leaky self-worth and fueling the pursuit this much more.

After years of enduring this chase for worth; anguished wrestling with my self; and much solution seeking from friends, books, and professionals, I experienced what might be considered an epiphany. I came to realize that my worth actually preceded my any and every thought and deed. Well, this changed everything. Now I reconfigured countless beliefs about myself, life, and others. Not a paradigm shift, a paradigm expansion. An awareness expansion as though a veil obscuring my awareness had been lifted. Knowing that my worth precedes my thoughts and deeds removes the need for perfection as I, you, and everyone is already fine from the beginning of life. I do wish I'd known this long ago. I imagine many different life choices, and yet, knowing and experiencing this pre-existing self-worth now, softens regret as well.

As an analogy for self-worth always being present, consider the moon up in the night sky. One night you look up in the starry sky and see only a sliver of a moon. Another week you look up in the night sky and see perhaps a half moon lit up and eventually a full moon shining down on you. Now if you did not know any better, you'd swear that the moon shrinks and expands through the month. But you know full well that the moon remains the same size night after night after night. The part of the moon that is illuminated varies, but the moon remains the same. It is the same situation with you and your worth. The only thing that changes is your awareness of it.

I am not and no human is perfect, yet we were made perfectly. Our very being stems from and is made up of worthiness. We could not exist otherwise. Knowing this, feeling this, and confirming this daily reminds me that I retain a constant and irrevocable worth. I can use it however I choose, with no risk to my worth. So many, if not all of life choice errors, dishonoring of self and others stem from the belief that we can or have already lost our worth. Verifying self-worth before taking any action naturally leads to positive constructive choices. I came to realize that I, you, every tree and every blade of grass and every rain drop and snowflake are already exactly perfect, as is.

———

Paraphrased from the unpublished manuscript, *The Myth of Original Sin; Remembering Aboriginal Unity* by John Burton, Ed.D.

∽

How You Feel Really Does Matter
Mandy Evans

Lots of people just plain flat out do not want to deal with their emotions. They don't want to feel them. They don't want to talk about them. Often they wish they would just go away.

No wonder. If you grew up human on Planet Earth, you probably learned early on that expressing your feelings led to trouble. Ever try squealing, laughing, and jumping for joy in a second-grade classroom? Or at the dinner table?

By third grade, most of us understood that it never pays to show anger at teachers or our heartbreak at being left out of a game at recess, or the total frustration of not being able to understand long division. We learned to hide, overcome, repress, suppress, and deaden our feelings any way we could, even if it took a large amount of alcohol, drugs, or hour after hour of mindless TV to do it. Day by day, we learned more rules about appropriate emotional responses and less and less about emotional freedom.

However, the feelings keep coming. For the first part of my life, I thought the way to change how I felt was to change the circumstances in my life. Most people I know learned the same approach. And so begins the endless struggle to improve everything! Lose weight, earn more money, get a better car, find your true love, get rid of your old true love, move to a bigger house.

Here's the lesson I think we should get early on: How you feel really does matter. How you feel is up to you.

Before you make a life-changing move in the hope of feeling better, always deal with your feelings first. Before you quit your job or leave your marriage in anger, find out about your anger. What is it about? Why is that the way you feel? Before you go on a diet, leave town, buy a new car, or get married so you can stop emotional pain, deal with your feelings first. You may still want to lose weight, get that car, or create a new adventure, but it will be a completely different experience with a far different outcome.

Because regardless of whether we like it, emotions are the rocket fuel of manifestation. We hear it from people who teach visualization techniques to overcome serious illnesses and from motivational speakers who command enormous corporate fees the word is out: Whatever it is you want to achieve, you've got to feel it first.

This mysterious law of the universe works regardless of whether you are aware of it, regardless of whether you believe it. Regardless of whether you are consciously aware of it, your emotional state always has and always will have a profound effect on what happens next in your life.

The choices you make and actions you take when you are afraid lead down a different road from the choices and actions you take when you are happy. The solutions you find to a problem when you feel guilty will not be the same ones you use when you feel at peace.

Feelings actually cause things to happen. Feelings influence events.

Getting, doing, having stuff is nice. Fame, fortune, and good looks stand out among the most popular getting-stuff goals. However, there is not a whole lot of correlation between getting stuff and the happiness that Madison Avenue, Hollywood, and Wall Street would have us believe it produces.

We all know people who stand out for their talent, financial achievement, beauty, or mighty deeds but are not happy.

The mind-boggling part is that they do not want to be happy—yet! They do not know that happiness is a real option for them and they do not know how to choose it.

Your emotional experience of life is so important. When we feel curious, grateful, loving, or happy, life seems like a precious gift. But if you are ridden with guilt, filled with fear, so angry that no love can enter your heart, or so resentful that joy is only an irritating word, then life is more like hell on earth. What good are fame, fortune, and good looks in hell?

As we wander about this paradise called Earth, the perception of what happens to us combines with our thoughts and beliefs about what life means. That ever-changing combination produces emotional responses. When we judge events and circumstances as good for us, we usually respond with some form of happiness. When we think bad things are happening we respond with anger, fear, guilt, sorrow, and the other so-called negative emotions.

What happens when you suspend that judgment? When life becomes a fascinating mystery, unfolding in the midst of infinite possibilities, you become more and more free to *choose* your feelings. You can allow more love, creativity, and joy into your life than you may have dreamed possible. Simply by asking yourself from time-to-time, "If I could feel any way I wanted to feel, what would it be?" You may come up with answers that will astound you.

Exercising your emotional options allows you to experience life on your own terms in the most real way possible. It's like magic. You can create the result first. You can be happy even before you change all of those things you want to change.

———

Mandy Evans is the author of *Emotional Options: A Handbook for Happiness* and *Traveling Free: How to Recover from the Past by Changing Your Beliefs*. For more information about her work and a free belief quiz, visit www.mandyevans.com.

Forgiveness
Jeremy Likness

One gift I wish I had received earlier in life is knowledge of forgiveness.

I spent much of my life carrying rusty anchors with me. It is difficult to move forward when we carry bitterness inside. I can laugh now about the times I held onto my grudges. I would literally bathe in poisonous thoughts. Now I realize those thoughts did nothing to the person I was holding a grudge against. It didn't bother them one bit. What it did was hold me back and prevent me from becoming my best.

Forgiveness isn't just about people. Sometimes we have trouble forgiving the things around us. I used to wake up in fear, angry at the universe. Starting the day in a fight or flight mode is a stressful way to begin the day. Perhaps I was worrying about the bills or angry about a car accident or some other event that appeared to be beyond my control.

When I found forgiveness, I quickly learned that forgiving is a process. I could not say, "I forgive" and then let go. Many of the anchors I carried with me were embedded deep within, so I had to constantly remind myself to toss them out. I would say, "I forgive and I release you" and imagine the face of the person I held a grudge against. It felt great. They went on with their own lives, but now I was free to live mine.

My next step was to forgive the world around me. I suddenly stopped blaming my misfortunes on the universe. Traffic happens. Rain happens. All of this is part of life. When I became friends with the universe (by not holding a grudge) the universe returned the gesture by providing abundance. This is when I started to learn about success, because success doesn't find selfish people. Not forgiving is a very selfish act. (If you think that having money is success, find a rich person who doesn't know how to forgive, and you might discover that being rich for them is nothing more than expensive unhappiness).

Then, in all my forgiving, I stumbled upon the greatest gift of all. I forgave myself! I learned that I could love myself and forgive myself for not being perfect. I used to be my own enemy. I now enjoy life and receive so much more—especially now that I can be friends with that reflection I see in the mirror.

———

Jeremy Likness is a health coach, motivational speaker, and author. Jeremy learned to forgive himself through the process of shedding 65 pounds of fat. Jeremy then became a Certified Fitness Trainer and Specialist in Performance Nutrition. He specializes in assisting others with releasing the thoughts that create overweight and obesity. See www.NaturalPhysiques.com.

∽

Logic Doesn't Exist

Logic doesn't exist. What we call logic is simply rationalization. After all, one person's totally logical argument often makes no sense to another person. If logic did exist, we would all agree. We don't. We don't buy the same cars, clothes, or houses, or vote for the same politicians or have the same philosophies about life. Yet we have perfectly logical reasons for everything we do, say, and believe.

Giving is like that. It defies logic. When you give anything, you tap into a higher spiritual law. You have little to do but give, wait, and receive. This may seem strange. Again, it's not logical. It's intuitive. It's spiritual. It's innate to the way the universe operates. All you have to do is get out of the way and let it cook.

Let me give you a story to illustrate my point: A person read one of my latest books, *The Greatest Money-Making Secret in History*, and decided to try giving. He saw an audio set he knew a friend of his wanted. He bought it. He gave it to his friend. It was a good deed. It could have ended there. But this giver then received an assignment worth over $117,000.

How is that possible?

It isn't possible, if you look at this event logically. A reasonable person could look at the giving and say it had nothing to do with the getting.

But what if you tossed logic out the window?

Take another example: Another person read my book and started giving. He wrote back saying: "My weekly income has gone up 113 percent in the last week. This is my best week, financially, of the year. New clients started calling me from all over the place. I've never had so many new customers in a week."

Did his giving lead to his increase?

You bet. Again, this defies logic. At least it defies human logic. We are so accustomed to giving and holding our hand out that giving with no expectation of return means we won't get a return. That's our logical argument, anyway. However, that isn't the case. Not in real life. Not here on planet Earth. When you give of yourself, you receive. Period.

What you're really asked to do when you give is trust. I wear an ancient Roman gold ring on my hand. It is estimated to be 2,500 years old. It has the word *Fidem* engraved on it, which is Latin for "Faith." It is a reminder to me to trust that when I give, I will receive—someday, someway, from someone. All I have to do is practice the principle.

It's the greatest money-making secret in history.

It's just not logical.

❦

How to Make a Decision

Few people know this, but any decision is acceptable when you can't decide.

The trick is to make the decision right *because* you made it.

In other words, when you are torn between two roads, pick one and then make the one you picked right.

In the grand scheme of things, it doesn't matter. If you can't see down the road enough to know which decision to make, then no one can fault you for making a decision.

Of course, in a pinch, you could always flip a coin.

～

You Will Always Want to Be Right and Rarely Will Be

Throughout your life, you will see people lie, steal, cheat, and maybe even kill in order to be right. This is built into your survival mechanism. The truth is, this mechanism is no longer necessary.

What is necessary in your life is to note what works and what doesn't work. Do your best to ignore being right, and focus instead on getting the results you want. Be willing to surrender habits and old ways of being in favor of new habits and new ways that lead you to your desired outcomes.

Said another way, you will want to be right in your arguments, but even if the other person stops arguing, they will still consider your viewpoint wrong. To them, they are right. To you, you are right. To the universe, you are both right.

You'll find happiness, peace, and faster routes to success when you give up being right.

Right?

～

Everything You Hear Isn't True

Don't believe everything you hear.

If you hear something positive about another, embrace it.

If you hear something negative about someone, be quiet. Observe. Learn the truth for yourself.

If you want to keep yourself in check, here's a helpful tip: Always talk about others as if they were in the same room with you, listening.

This technique will give you immediate perspective on what you should and should not be saying.

Judgment Is Not Evil
Bruce M. Burns

I've heard many people choose not to judge as if judgment is some form of evil. It is important to remember the difference between judgment (gloating over someone else's inadequacies or differences) and discrimination. The discriminating eater chooses specific, healthy foods for their well-being. Eating a salad is not a judgment of gravity-challenged individuals. It is a self-sustaining choice. If you do not wish to be around smokers and their smoke—discriminating in such a way that keeps you smoke free isn't a judgment about smokers—it is a demonstration of one's courage to choose for self.

Names Do Hurt

Along the course of your life you'll hear the phrase, "Sticks and stones may break my bones but names will never hurt me."

It's a lie.

In many ways, names will hurt far more, and the pain lasts far longer, than any stick or stone.

Predicting the End of the World Will Make You Look Bad

People throughout history have predicted the world's end. They've all been wrong. No exceptions. None.

A word to the wise: Though you may at times feel the world should end, it won't. So rather than being a messenger of doom and gloom, which won't win you any friends or make you feel good, be a yea-sayer. Predict the world will last a long time.

It will, at least longer than your own lifetime.

❧

All Time Happens Now

Time is an illusion.

Although you may never be able to wrap your head around this concept, all time happens right now.

The past is gone. You remember it now, and you remember it inaccurately, but the past is gone.

The future hasn't happened yet, and when it gets here, it will be now.

All that happened before, and all that will happen, are illusions.

The only thing that matters, the only thing that is real, is now.

❧

What Time Is It For?

I was reading *The Architecture of All Abundance* by Lenedra Carroll, mother of the singer Jewel. She advises you to ask yourself, "What is it time for?"

It means, right now, what is there for you to do?

What is appropriate, falling into place, ready to hatch?

Rather than forcing what you want to happen, see *what wants* to be done now.

What is it time for?

Most things self-correct in time.

—LARRY ANDREWS

OPTIMUM PERFORMANCE

❧

Getting the Best Out of Your Life

Indian Wisdom: Two Wolves

An elder Cherokee was teaching his grandchildren. He said to them:

"A fight is going on inside me. It is a terrible fight. It is between two wolves: One wolf represents fear, anger, envy, sorrow, regret, greed, arrogance, self-pity, guilt, resentment, inferiority, lies, false pride, superiority, and ego. The other stands for joy, peace, love, hope, sharing, serenity, humility, kindness, benevolence, friendship, empathy, generosity, truth, compassion, and faith. This same fight is going on inside you, and inside every other person, too."

They thought about it for a minute, then one child asked his grandfather:

"Which wolf will win?"

The old Cherokee simply replied . . . "The one you feed."

Don't Be Afraid to Ask for Help

Most people want to do things by themselves, to feel good about themselves and their accomplishments. Although ultimately you will do things by yourself, asking for help is not a sign of weakness. Great people are always willing to lend a hand to those who ask for help out of a sincere desire to grow and change for the better. Whether you need directions or a loan, don't be afraid to ask for help.

To Change, Burn Your Bridges

At some point in your life you will decide you want to change something, whether it is to quit smoking (which you should never have started), or quit drinking, or quit overeating, or whatever. However, saying, "I want to change" isn't enough to actually change. Yes, it's the beginning of the process, but it will stop there if you don't go to the next step.

The next step is to burn your bridges. Make it impossible to go back to the old habit or way of being. This may mean creating an uncomfortable scenario if you fail. In other words, if you say you will lose 25 pounds by the end of the season or donate your car to a person or cause you don't like, you have leveraged yourself for success.

The lesson here is that you can motivate yourself for change with a decision and with the leverage to succeed. Create a win-win for yourself, knowing that you cannot not fail, because your bridges have been burned.

What to Do When You Are Afraid
Dr. Larina Kase

I have learned an important life lesson both personally and through my training as a psychologist. Although I learned it by accident initially, it is one that works much better when you do it on purpose. I will tell you about it so you can look for ways to purposefully do things differently to reduce fear, improve happiness, and increase your chances of success in your life's endeavors.

Here is the lesson: *Whenever you are afraid, uncomfortable, nervous, or worried, do the opposite of what you would naturally do.*

Fear is one of the most common human emotions. We all have things that we are afraid of. Many children worry about going to school or are afraid of animals or new activities. Adults commonly fear public speaking, interpersonal conflicts, flying, and many other things that we perceive as threatening or potentially embarrassing.

The common response to fear is to try to reduce it. If your child is anxious, you are naturally going to help him or her to feel better. By this process, people learn to avoid experiencing fear. Although this is the natural response, it is also the least helpful response.

The more you avoid experiencing anxiety, the more your discomfort will grow over time. You will avoid facing your fear and eventually miss out on many important activities because you are living within your comfort zone. You will also miss out on learning that when you do allow yourself to experience the anxiety, it naturally goes away on its own.

My message to you is to push yourself to get out of the comfort zone you may be living in. You will then enter the place where your most tremendous personal and professional success will begin.

This is true in many areas of life. Think about when you first started dating someone. You may have had butterflies and nervousness. If you had avoided these feelings, you may have missed out on a wonderful relationship. You may have been uncomfortable with speaking up in class or at work. Yet when you confronted your anxieties, over time your confidence grew and your fear shrunk.

When you feel anxious or uncomfortable, tell yourself that those feelings are wonderful because that means you are pushing yourself to get over your fears, fully experience life, and become a more confident and complete human being.

———

Dr. Larina Kase, President of Performance and Success Coaching, LLC, coauthored the e-book, *End Self-Sabotage*, at www.endselfsabotage.com.

❧

My Inherited Fear of Financial Ruin
Dr. Robert Anthony

For many years I struggled with money issues. It wasn't until later in life that I realized why.

I was raised in a family where money was always an issue. Actually, the issue was the *lack* of money—especially for my father.

My father was raised as an only child in a poor Italian immigrant family. When the Great Depression hit in 1929, my grandparents, like many other people, lost their life savings because the banks closed down without notice, leaving them virtually broke. At that time there was no FDIC insurance to protect the money you had in the bank.

They also lived in a cold climate on the East Coast. During those days, most homes were heated by coal furnaces. In order to heat their home my father would have to go to the railroad tracks where the trains brought the coal to the coal yard and he would pick up the pieces of coal that fell off the railroad cars. This is the only way they could afford to heat their house.

During that time, life was so difficult for my father and my grandparents that years later, even when things improved and my father was financially comfortable, he never got over the Great Depression. He relived the Great Depression in his mind every day for the rest of his life!

When I was growing up, all my father talked about was the fact that there is never enough so you have to earn as much money as possible. And worse yet, we always need to be on the lookout for an impending danger that will take away all our money.

So what do you suppose became my reality about money?

There's never enough.

I have to earn as much as possible to protect myself against loss.

There is a good chance I will eventually lose what I have.

Now here is the sad part. Even after I became an adult and earned enough at my profession (an amount that most people would consider very substantial) I still didn't have enough. No matter how much I earned, I was always just getting by. And of course, I was afraid I would lose what I had—which I *did* on several occasions!

As you can see, I inherited my father's money issues. Unfortunately, we all inherit our parents' issues about money unless we consciously change them. Now, looking back, it is so clear why I kept myself broke.

I brought this belief system *from* my childhood *into* the rest of my life, and I didn't even see what I was doing! Don't get me wrong. I was always motivated to try to make a lot of money, but I was always operating out of the mentality that There isn't enough and I will eventually lose what I have.

And guess what? That was my reality. The Law of Cause and Effect or the Attractor Factor was at work, and I didn't even know it! It was my truth, so no matter how long and hard I worked, I always ended up with the same result.

No matter how much money I earned—and trust me, it was a lot—I either just got by, or managed to lose it. And all the time I was worrying about how I was going to make *more* money.

What is important to understand here is that my motivation for making money was based on my fear of not having enough and losing what I had.

So, as embarrassing as it is to admit, I lived this way for over 40 years of my life—40! And the part that is the most embarrassing is that I was in the business of helping people to become successful, yet I was a financial failure.

Here I was thinking, talking about, and working toward wealth and studying success, but financial success was just out of my reach. The end result was that my dominant thoughts prevailed.

Keep in mind, I didn't consciously do this to myself. However, while all this was going on, I blamed my parents, poor business decisions, my mate, the government, and extenuating circumstances for my lack of financial success.

Well, finally I was fortunate to learn the most important life lesson I have ever learned—*we attract whatever we focus on, or said another way, we become what we think about all day long.*

What most people do not understand is that we do not attract what we want, we attract what we *focus on*. Almost everyone desires more money in their lives, so obviously *wanting* it is not the key to *having* it.

If you are currently experiencing anxiety, scarcity, depression, or an inability to attract what you desire, you must take a look at how you have been attracting these things into your life. You must look at the attractor pattern for these things. These things show up in your life because you have been consciously or unconsciously focusing on them.

If you still do not have what you want, then you are not creating a vibrational match. Simply put, you are focusing on what you *don't* want instead of what you *do* want. *All the obstacles you face in life are the result of a vibrational mismatch.* Until you decide to consciously connect with a higher vibrational level, you will remain stuck where you are.

So here is the secret—*If you change the way you look at things, the things you look at will change.*

So how do you look at life? Your life is essentially based on what you believe to be true about yourself. This determines your level of expectations. These expectations are based on your belief in limitations, scarcity and pessimism about what is possible for you.

These beliefs form the basis of how you look at life, and that perception creates what you experience. So what you have or don't have or what you can create or cannot create will be determined by your limiting viewpoints of impossibility.

The source energy within you is limitless. And because you are one with this source energy or the universal creative mind, the possibilities for you are also limitless. However, this source energy can only work *with you* and *for you* when you are in *harmony* with it.

Source energy or the universal creative mind is in a constant state of supplying everything we can possibly imagine. It takes orders 24/7. It never shuts down, never takes a holiday, sick leave, or any days off. It is perpetually there to take orders and supply what you have asked for.

If this is true, then why are some people able to access this flow while others feel separated from it? The answer is simple. If it is always giving what we ask for and you are experiencing shortages in your life, then you are creating *resistance* to allowing it to come into your life.

You are placing resistance in the way of the natural flow of whatever you desire. If the universe is based on the laws of energy and attraction, which means everything is vibrating at a particular frequency, then you are vibrating at a frequency that is in contradiction to what you desire.

This is why I had so many financial problems for over 40 years. It had nothing to do with money. I was not in vibrational harmony with what I desired. Instead, I was creating resistance to what I desired, while trying to attract it at the same time.

Thoughts that emphasize lack, limitation, fear, scarcity, or unworthiness set up a contradiction in energy. The contradiction creates a field of *disallowing*. In essence, you are out of harmony with your desires.

Remember, you are part of the universal creative mind. If you put yourself into a nonresistant state of mind, which means you are in harmony with your desires, then source energy or the universal creative mind will work in harmony with your desires. It has no choice in the matter. It can only act upon your thoughts and feeling that have no vibrational contradiction to your desire.

You don't need to get overwhelmed by this. In fact, you really don't need to change anything. Instead, say to yourself, "The one thing I have control over is my own thoughts about allowing what I desire to come into my life right now. More importantly it doesn't matter what I have thought before, or for how long, or how many pressures I am under at the moment. Instead I am going to stop generating more contradictory thoughts today—one at a time."

You do this by affirming that, "I can create anything I desire because I refuse to allow anything or anyone that is not in harmony with my desire to run my life. I allow whatever I desire to come into my life right now."

When you activate this thought enough times, it will become a habit, and it will eliminate your resistance to allowing your desire to manifest itself in your life. As you practice this path of least resistance, it is no longer something you *choose*, it is something that you *are*. This is when the miracles begin to happen. And, they will *continue* to happen for the rest of your life as long as you focus on what you want instead of what you don't want.

So don't waste 40 years of your life creating in reverse. Instead learn from this life lesson and you will open the door to abundance for the rest of your life.

————

Dr. Robert Anthony is a legend in personal development and author of many books including *Beyond Positive Thinking*.

∾

Are You Playing the Role of Victim?
Nerissa Oden

Are you playing the role of victim? How would you even know if you were playing that role if you were reared that way from birth? Ask yourself these six questions:

1. Are the cards stacked against you?
2. Are you plagued by bad luck?
3. Were/Are you held back from succeeding?
4. Does your work mostly go unnoticed?
5. Was modern society set up by a privileged few?
6. Does society disrespect you and your kind?

If you answered yes to any of these questions, you *are* playing the role of victim. Get a Grip.

Throughout human history there has been an unequal distribution of power and inheritances. The thing to remember is that people can overcome any mass inequality at the individual level.

For example, women have always fought in wars next to men, become business owners, even cultural icons, and all the while during times when these things were culturally forbidden, even illegal. Women who achieved these goals did so by posing as men. Most were never discovered or written about, but enough were discovered (most upon their death) to forge a new reality. These women saw an opportunity and took it. They didn't let anything like clothing or sex interfere with their dream of freedom and equality.

Many of you might have just said, "But I am a different color or handicapped (or this or that) and I am more easily identified than a woman with her breasts bound."

Victim.

There are many, many more stories of success at the individual level: gay couples posing as relatives and living together their whole lives, African-Americans that escaped and relocated, children who overcame cruel parents, and more.

So before you choose to be a lifelong victim, ask yourself, "Where are my opportunities? Should I relocate? Should I pick better friends? Find a better job? Go back to school? Get a roommate to save money? What does my intuition say? Talk to my family more? Talk to my family less?"

And I'm sure you can think of many more questions that will help guide you to self-betterment and get you closer to your goals. Listen to your heart and make choices that actively serve to better yourself. Anything less is choosing to live as a victim. You are the only one who can choose the life you live.

———

Nerissa Oden is a video editor and author. See www.thevideoqueen.com.

How to Get a Job

Let the beauty we love be what we do.
   —JELALUDDIN RUMI, thirteenth century Sufi poet and mystic

Be willing to work for free.

Mark Twain advised it.

Many successful people got their first jobs by being an apprentice. They basically said, "I'll work for you for free for two months. If you like me, hire me. If you don't, let me go."

Another way to get a job is to be less concerned about what it is. Look around and you'll see work. It may not be what you want, but it's a start.

Numerous famous and wealthy people began as bus boys, cooks, and taxi drivers.

Many people came to this country with no money, no job, no ability to speak the language, and yet went on to create fortunes.

There is work.

Accept it and you have your first job.

❧

Get a Pet

Having a pet can lower your blood pressure and release your stress. It can also open your heart and teach you love.

Of course, having a pet could increase your blood pressure and increase your stress, so choose your pet wisely.

I know a woman who loves exotic animals. Her first panther led to chimpanzees, zebras, wombats, and more. And this hobby led to her opening a safari. People come from all over the country to see her exotic collection.

Of course, if raising a baboon sounds stressful to you, then consider owning a turtle.

❧

Illness Is a Call from Your Body

You don't need to get sick.

Years ago I got the flu. When I spoke to a healer about it, he pointed out that getting the flu meant you wanted to flee or run away from something. I thought about it and realized I wanted to flee my job at the time. Once I realized I had created my illness to make an excuse for not working, I could no longer get the flu again.

Most likely, all illnesses are like that. You'll create them to get your attention. They'll become a metaphor for something in your life.

For example, one time I was angry about what a friend was doing. Shortly after that I got a boil on my chest. It was full of pus and needed to be opened and released.

How much more relevant can you get? I was boiling over with anger. I was full of pus over my friend's behavior. It manifested itself on my body.

Whenever you get ill, look for the hidden reason for the illness. Most likely, once you find it, the illness will vanish.

❧

Pay Your Taxes

As a citizen in the country where you live, you will be asked to contribute to the government's expenses. You'll resent this and resist this, at least at first, but ultimately you'll have to pay.

If you enjoy numbers and laws, you may want to learn about ways to save money on your taxes. If you don't enjoy the subjects, then consider hiring someone who does.

Either way, pay your taxes. You'll find life easier.

❧

The Favorite Question of Your Mind Can Drive You Batty

What is the favorite question of your mind?

Few realize this, but it is simply, "What if?"

Your mind asks, "What if this happens, or that?" as a way to control you, to make you afraid. It will run circles around you and keep you jailed unless you ignore it.

When your mind asks, "What if?" and plays a negative movie in your mind, change it by asking, "What if?" and play a positive scenario.

As always, you are in control (but you may forget that a lot throughout your life).

SPECIFICATIONS

~

What You Need to Know About Others

People Idolize the Past, Complain about the Present, and Fear the Future

I often hear people say we live in stressful times today. A quick look at history, however, reveals that we are richer, healthier, and happier now than at any time in world history, ever. Yet we all long for the good old days. And we all complain about the present and fear the future. If you want to make more friends or sales, tie your product to the nostalgia of the past, or urge people to buy now to solve the agony of the present, or convince them that your business will make the uncertain future less risky. Until more people are enlightened, and realize that now is the point of power and the moment of greatest joy, you can increase your happiness by playing to what people already believe.

People Never Question Their Own Beliefs, so Don't Try to Change Them

Socrates encouraged us to know ourselves, but most people don't realize they are fish in a pool of water. They don't question being a fish or see the water. We are all in a trance of one sort or another, believing we are doctors, lawyers, salespeople, or what have you. The deepest beliefs our parents gave us are rarely questioned. To awaken, question all.

❧

People Will Tend to Say Yes If You Start Them Saying Yes

Popular stage magician C. J. Johnson and I were having lunch. He told me he had a great idea for a new headline. It was, "Do you make as much money performing magic as your neighbors make with their real jobs?" I told C. J. I liked the headline but wanted him to change it so it could only be answered with a yes. His existing question could be answered with a no, which would put his prospects into a no mindset. I suggested C. J. change his headline to read, "Would you like to make as much money performing magic as your neighbors make with their real jobs?" Now people can say yes and get into a yes mindset. Once there, they will tend to say yes once you ask them to buy. You can use this principle in everyday conversation, when looking for a date, as well as in business presentations, or anything else.

❧

People Do Things Only for the Good Feelings They Get

Think about it. Why did you buy the new car? Or the new dress? Or the new tool set? You bought it because on some level the item would make you feel better. My life partner just bought a new lawn mower. She would probably never admit that buying it made her feel better, but the truth is, not buying it would make her feel worse. Keep both sides of this insight in mind when trying to sell to people. Remind them of what happens if they don't buy (continued pain) and remind them of what happens when they do buy (pleasure). Focus on those good feelings and you'll increase sales. Remember, even if you aren't in sales, you are always selling. You are selling yourself, your ideas, your personality, your beliefs, and so forth.

People Will Pay Any Amount of Money to Have Their Inner States Changed

People aren't happy. They have a desperate, black, sinking feeling within themselves that silently gnaws at them, saying, "Life can be better than this." They'll pay any amount of money to feel better, often illegally. They'll line up to take terrifying rides on roller coasters or sit in theaters to watch horror flicks and scream in fear. They'll pay you to help them feel anything other than what they feel right now. When you serve them, treat them like royalty. When you sell them a product, make sure it is offered as fun, unique, or controversial. Change their inner state and they will make you rich.

People Want to Be Happy–Period

Thoreau said it best when he said the mass of men (he meant women, too, I'm sure) lead lives of quiet desperation. I learned many years ago that, more than anything else in the world, people want to be happy. When I go to any place of business, if the clerk or owner or person on the phone is up-beat and friendly and makes me feel up-beat and happy, they'll get my repeat business. How can you help people feel happy? Treat them with respect, show your humor, radiate your own happiness, and you'll attract more sales and win more friends.

People Respond to Flattery

You are really smart to be reading this. Few people are wise enough or aware enough to invest in a book like this to help them lead a happier life. You're the exception. And like everyone else, you like to think you're smart, hip, sexy, popular, and other positive traits. Note how you felt when you began reading this paragraph. Didn't you feel good as you read, "You are really smart to be reading this"? Didn't you also feel good about me for noting how smart you are? Everyone responds to flattery: You, me, everyone.

❧

People Will Never Argue with You If You Never Make Them Wrong

When someone calls you and complains, listen. Don't argue. Don't make them wrong. As long as you can remain neutral, you will resolve the issue and win a friend. This same principle works in every aspect of your life. It may be a challenge to do, because you have to keep your ego in check. You'll want to be right. Regardless of whether you are, be quiet. You'll win the argument if you don't argue. Besides, arguing just escalates the argument. Neither of you will win, and you'll lose a customer or friend or mate for life.

❧

People Always Act for Positive Reasons, Even If the Behavior Is Negative

Some of these truisms are tough to swallow. People always act for positive reasons. *Always?* Yes, always. No exceptions. Even the person who is hurting another is in some way crying out, in the only way he or she knows, to be heard or to express something. The person isn't wrong; their behavior is.

Closer to home, an employee who doesn't do his job may still be doing the best he can; the customer who routinely complains may still be doing the best he or she can. The children who keep getting into trouble may still be doing the best they can.

The point is to not condemn the person at all and to separate out what they do. Focus on their activity, don't judge them, and you'll keep your life afloat. People work perfectly. When what they do doesn't work perfectly for you, find out what the person needs to achieve, what they are trying to get, and help them get it.

❧

People Will Respond to You If You Get Out of Your Ego and into Theirs

Who would you rather talk about today, me or you?

I'm betting you'd much prefer to talk about yourself.

When someone shows you a group photograph of your family, whose face do you look for first? Yours, of course.

When you are talking to prospects, writing to customers, or in any way interacting with people, focus on them and you'll increase your sales and deepen your friendships. Why? Because people quite naturally are interested in themselves first. It's not wrong.

In fact, it's a key to your wealth.

❧

People Want to Be Recognized

Carl Stevens is a famous sales person, author, speaker, and trainer. He once told me that he entered and won a sales contest, not for the trip to Hawaii that the winner would receive, but for the attention he got from his peers for being the best sales person they had.

Stroking egos can be a big money maker for you. Recognize your customers, family, and friends. One year the first birthday card I received from anyone was from Radio Shack. That was five years ago. I was never a fan of them until that moment.

Acknowledge your customers, family, and friends, and you can keep them for life.

❧

People Universally Feel Deprived

Few of us are satisfied. We feel cheated by life. We expect more and feel deprived when we don't get it. We are much like babies in adult bodies. To make more money, help people feel fulfilled. Serve them. Cherish them. Give them more than what they expect. Surprise them with little gifts, notes, or even visits. Show you care.

❦

People Are Collectors of Something, Whether of Books, Thimbles, or Recipes, Though They May Deny It

I told this truism to a friend and he said, "Yeah, people are funny, but I sure don't collect anything." Yet on his shelf was every video in the James Bond 007 series. If you want a quick way to get rich, find out what a specific group of people are collecting and sell them something in that same category. Write a booklet about 007 and you may get my friend's money. Find people who already buy weight-loss products and you can probably sell them another weight-loss product. Although they would never admit it, they collect weight-loss products in the hope that one of them will work one day.

❦

People Will Continue with a Bad Habit until It Hurts

It takes a lot for people to change—usually a lot of pain. Don't expect to see anyone change soon, but do expect to sell them ways to change easily. Sell them the dream, and they will likely buy. Tell them it will take hard work, and they will rarely buy, even if that's the truth. Respect the fact that people will continue to smoke, drink, overeat, or whatever they think their bad habit is, and continue to offer them workable solutions. They'll buy, and one day, they may even change.

❦

People Will Do Whatever You Want as Long as They Don't Have a Counterthought to Your Request. Handle the Objection and They Will Comply

Hypnotists know this. They cannot get you to do something that goes against your core values and beliefs—not unless they change those core values and beliefs. Your friends, family, and prospects are the same. If they want to buy your product, they will do so. If they have any concerns, they won't buy until you resolve those issues. The best thing to do is handle objections before they come up. Then, when you ask them to buy, or to go out with you, they will comply.

❧

People Feel That Someone Else Is in Control and Desperately Seek Ways to Have Power Again

How many times a day do you hear yourself and others complain about *them* or *they*? "They won't let us park there" or "Their new rules suck." This unnamed power makes people feel impotent. As a result, they are eager to feel in control. Offer them a way to have more power, to beat the system, and you'll have their attention.

❧

People Will Follow Commands That Make Them Feel Superior

You are part of a small group of people. This group is highly intelligent, perceptive, and on the leading edge of growth.

How does that make you feel? Don't you feel a sense of pride?

How do you feel about me, now that you know that I realize you are one of the superior people in the world? Don't you think I'm pretty smart for being so perceptive? Yes, I've flattered you. (Remember the fact that people respond to flattery is another truism). However, I also have some power over you. Now that I have your respect, I'd like you to visit one of my web sites. Better yet, why not go to amazon.com and order my latest book? You, as a leader in the world today, can appreciate the importance of reading even the most controversial material. It's the superior thing to do, and only superior people will go do it right now.

∽

People Are Deeply Affected by What Others Think

Most people can't decide to do something on their own. They need to know what the rest of the world thinks. To sell or convince any-one of anything, deliver a long line of endorsements—testimonials from real people who have experienced real results. By the same to-ken, keep your service and quality top notch. People will talk about you behind your back. Unless you and your word are impeccable, the word will get out that you are to be avoided. Again, people won't decide totally alone if you are valuable or not; they will look to their family, friends, coworkers, and peers to tell them what to think. Help people to think about you the way you want them to think about you by giving them quotes from people that make you look good.

∽

People Only Act for Self-Serving Reasons, No Matter What They Say or What You Think

Everyone disagrees with this truism. Still, it's true. No one does anything without a secret desire to benefit from what they are do-ing. Even the most altruistic among us is behaving in a way that makes them feel better. If you want to sell more of anything, tie your goods to what people want. People will donate more money to any cause, for example, if you give them something with their names on it. People will buy your product or service if it strokes their ego, even subtly. Face it. You do it, too. You gave money and didn't get any-thing in return? Baloney. You *felt* better or you wouldn't have done it. Feeling better was your payoff. Again, play to people's egos, and you can win friends and get rich.

People Unconsciously Respond to Your Unconscious Intentions

This is a principle from my book, *The Attractor Factor*. It means that your unconscious desires affect other people. In a way, you train people to respond to you by what you say and don't say. I was on the phone with Bob Proctor. He said, "Your energy goes out and touches the person you are talking to while you are talking to them."

That means that if you have a self-sabotaging desire in you, or if you are trying to pull a fast one on people, or if you don't believe in your own business, your prospects will sense it. They will respond to your unconscious. If you want to get more business, get clear. Be congruent. Be sure you totally believe in yourself, your business, and your customer's good will.

People Will Never Change Their Human Emotions or Basic Desires—Only Their Dress and Their Tools Will Change

People throughout time have been motivated by the same desires and emotions. The top three goals of everyone alive are food, love, and money. They were the same in the 1700s and will be the same in the 2700s. What changes are customs and technology. Humans remain human. Appeal to their basic self-interests—help them achieve food, love, and money, for example—and they'll help you get at least one of your goals, too.

PROPER USAGE

❧

Defining Your Life's Purpose

✌

You Can Have Whatever You Want
As Long As You Don't Want It

You'll learn in life that needing is an addiction that pushes away whatever you want. As long as you want something without needing it, you can have it. As soon as you need it, you send out a signal that will push it away. This is an advanced concept, so don't get a head cramp if it doesn't make sense just yet.

✌

Rags to Rages
Mark Joyner

When I was a young punk rocker in Reno, NV, one of my heroes was a local legend by the name of Tony Hospital. We called him Hospital because his crazy skateboarding and surfing antics always had him in and out of one.

One day he came over to my house to get a haircut (cutting punk rock hair is not hard and we did it for each other often). He asked me to shave the word *rage* into his head, and I inadvertently ran out of space so it said *rag*. For a brief moment, I thought Tony would kick my ass (this man truly had zero fear), so I hesitantly handed him the mirror.

He looked at it and said, "Rag. Cool. Rag," got up, picked up his skateboard, and started skating in front of my house.

He had no fear, but he wasn't a cruel man. He had a big heart and was in love with life.

Other people would have been angry or embarrassed, but Tony simply turned it into something good, got up, and skated on.

That moment always affected me deeply. Never have I been able to be so unaffected and internally unstoppable, but I've strived for it every day of my life.

Later on I discovered that Tony had become addicted to shooting heroin. He got his girlfriend hooked as well and she eventually OD'd and died.

On the one year anniversary of her death Tony took his own life.

I used to think that simply living with passion and letting nothing affect you was the key to life, but it seems Tony took it too far. Or perhaps to the wrong place.

At this point I'm tempted to wax philosophical about how our passions can just as easily fuel destruction as well as creation. I could refer to the golden mean and preach to you balance, but what is all that other than self-indulgent prattle?

I won't pretend to understand how or why this happened to him. What's important for your life is to know that it did. Nothing more.

———

Mark Joyner is an Internet celebrity and best-selling author. His latest book is *The Irresistible Offer*. See www.mrfire.simpleology.com.

❧

Crazy Wisdom
Blair Warren

First, realize that no one has ever done a great thing. Not written a great novel, painted a great painting or even cooked a great meal. Anything we do, if it is to *ever* be deemed great, must be deemed great *after the fact*, not during the creation itself. Furthermore, other people, *not creators themselves*, bestow the label *great*.

What I mean by this is that it is tempting to think that people who have created great works of art *knew* they were doing so and that their experience of creation must be dramatically different than our own. The truth is, Hemingway simply put words on paper, one after the other, just like the rest of us. Michelangelo put paint down one stroke at a time, just like the rest of us. Their works only became great when they were finished and other people deemed them great.

This is a very freeing thought for me when I am frustrated at the way my writing is going. When I remind myself that even great writers went through what I am going through, it encourages me to go on.

My second idea is this: It is critical to understand the difference between an illusion and the one who *makes* the illusion. For example, when I was a kid, I worshiped the rock star Gene Simmons of KISS. I wanted to be just like him and did everything I could to make that happen. The trouble was, I was emulating an illusion. It turns out Gene Simmons wasn't the blood-spitting, fire-breathing rebel I saw on stage. That was all an act. It was only years later that I learned the truth. He was an educated, conservative man who never touched drugs or alcohol in his life. I felt like such an idiot. But I was only thirteen at the time and believed everything I saw. I shudder to think how differently my life might have turned out had I known the truth and emulated the illusion maker and not the illusion.

———

Blair Warren is a TV producer and author. See www.BlairWarren.com.

Be who you are, honestly, truthfully, and entirely. There is no one who can be you better.

—Fourteen-year-old HARMONY MCCORMICK-WITSTYN

❧

Growing Old May Be a Choice

Many scientists are baffled and have no idea why we age, considering that our bodies are constantly regenerating themselves.

So then, why do we age?

Bad diet/poor health choices (drinking, smoking, etc.), stress, our deep rooted beliefs/programming that aging is normal and the biggest factor of all: the baggage that we drag around with us every day makes us old.

Aging may be unnecessary and should be classified as being a disease, rather than something that is a normal part of life.

This isn't going to be easy to accept, because the majority of the world looks around, sees people aging and dying, and assumes that is the way it is.

But that's not normal.

❧

Money Is Energy

Money is neutral.

In life you will find people that will die for it or kill for it, but in the end, they went after something that is, in and of itself, meaningless.

Money is an innocent means of exchange. It replaces trading tomatoes for shoes. It simplifies the bartering process.

Money is energy and means nothing.

What you do with money and why you want it are what counts.

❧

Marketing Is Not Evil

Yesterday I met a rancher who raises buffalo and sells bison products. He gushed facts. For example, I didn't know buffalo never get cancer. Or that buffalo meat is leaner, healthier, and better for you than any other red meat. I also didn't know that buffalo contains fewer calories than even chicken.

"Most people just don't know how to cook it," the rancher explained. "Since the meat is lean, it needs to be slowly cooked on a really low flame."

He went on to add:

"People on the Paleo Diet, sometimes called the caveman diet, really love it. It helps them lose weight and get trim naturally," he said. "I eat one to two pounds of bison every day, some veggies, and I'm fit and strong."

I was so taken by this new information that I placed a large order on the spot.

But the rancher also had some opinions that made me curious.

"I'm just a rancher," he told me. "I run my ranch by myself and I work night and day, yet at the end of it all, I have to go out and market this stuff. I almost hate it."

"You hate marketing?" I asked.

"I just saw the actor Billy Bob Thornton on television and he said, 'Marketing is evil.'"

"That's interesting," I countered. "The reason Thornton is on television is because he is marketing the latest movie he's in."

"Well, I don't like marketing," the rancher told me. "Maybe it's because I don't know how to do it."

At this point, Nerissa came out and met the rancher, too. He offered her a sample of the buffalo jerky he made. He held it out in front of her and said, "You'll eat this and you won't want anything else the rest of the day. This is the most filling and satisfying food you'll ever have," he said. "There are no preservatives and it's all natural."

Of course, at that point I wanted some jerky, too.

When the rancher went to write up our order, he pulled out of his truck a beautiful notebook. He started to place it on the hood of my BMW Z3 sports car when I stopped him.

"I don't want it scratched," I said.

"Look at this," he said, rubbing the leather on the notebook. "Go ahead and touch it and see how smooth it is."

I did. The leather was melted-butter-soft.

The rancher then asked me something hypnotic: "Can you imagine walking into a meeting with one of these under your arm?"

Of course, that question activated the visual part of my brain and engaged my ego. I instantly wanted the unusual product.

"How can I get one of those?" I asked.

"I can have one made for you, if you want."

I ordered one of the buffalo notebooks, too.

I then paid the rancher, shook his hand, and he got in his truck, still muttering that he didn't like marketing. He said he was so behind in learning marketing that he was prehistoric in his practices.

"Guess you're doing Paleo Marketing," I offered.

He laughed and drove off.

He didn't seem to notice that his nonmarketing made a lot of sales that day. I bought meat, jerky, and a notebook. I also bought a case of honey, which I forgot to mention. None of it was cheap, either.

I've said it before and I'll say it again: Marketing is simply engagingly informing the people most likely to be interested in your product or service that it's available.

This is what I teach people in my Executive Mentoring Program. I'll repeat it: Marketing is simply engagingly informing the people most likely to be interested in your product or service that it's available.

It's not about manipulation.

It's about information.

The more passionately and sincerely you convey your information, the more hypnotic your marketing will be.

But if you try to market your business to someone who has no interest in it, you may be considered evil.

That rancher was marketing, though he'd never admit it. His love for his product was apparent. He eats buffalo, wears buffalo, raises buffalo, and talks buffalo. He doesn't talk bull, he talks buffalo. And when he talks, if the people listening are at all interested in bison, they buy.

Marketing is only evil when you lie or mislead people to make a sale, or when your message isn't appropriate for the audience you reached. No one should ever do that. Ever. There's no excuse for it.

If you're offering a product or service you believe in, then share your excitement for it to the right audience. (If you don't believe in your product or service, what are you doing trying to sell it?)

Said another way, if you have something that would truly benefit a certain group of people, and you don't tell them, aren't you doing them a disservice?

Again, marketing is basically sharing your love, your passion, your belief. When you share it with someone who welcomes it, more often than not, it leads to a sale, naturally, easily, effortlessly.

And that's no BS.

Failure Is Not Death

A famous businessman once said, "I'm 74 years old and a million-aire now, but I had to try a lot of things and fail at a lot of things to get here. Here's what I learned about failure: Nothing bad ever happens to you."

Nothing bad ever happens to you.

There it is. It's the secret to handling failure. You go on to the next thing. You don't give up. You take a deep breath. You dust yourself off. You learn.

And you do the next thing.

Failure is not death.

How to Handle Death

If you're the one who died, you don't need this section.

If you lost someone close to you, rejoice that they have moved to their next adventure.

It's okay to miss them.

It's okay to cry.

Grieving is part of the life experience.

It will last as long as it lasts.

You're still okay.

The Only Thing You Can Count On

We just got back from a trip to Houston, where we attended the memorial service for my ex-wife and best friend of 27 years, Marian.

It stormed the entire three-hour drive there. The city was flooding, the sky dark, the clouds dumping their rain, the streets crowded and dangerous. Yet a few dozen people weathered the storm and attended the service. Some people I hadn't seen in 15 years. Some I've known for 30 years. Some I never met before, and only knew through stories Marian told me. It was a warm, loving, intimate group, all with one thing in common: their love for Marian.

David, Marian's best friend over the last few years, stood and read parts from Marian's unpublished and unfinished auto-biography. He wanted to show that this loving woman had gone through hell as a child, yet somehow learned to love unconditionally.

Stories about Marian's mean grandmother and cold father reminded me of why Marian wanted to commit suicide as a young woman in Oregon. Fortunately, she didn't, and she enjoyed over 30 more years of life's sunshine.

I didn't plan to speak at the service. After four days of emotional misery, bawling my eyes out in private, missing my beloved of almost three decades, I didn't think I could stand, let alone speak, but I surprised myself. I got up, went to the podium, and fumbled to say the following: "David left out one thing," I began. "He forgot to tell you the title of Marian's life story. She called it 'It's All Good.'"

I went on to say that even through the pain she had suffered—her unhappy childhood, her near-fatal car accident two years previously, the molestation by her therapist, her struggles with self-esteem and more—she always looked for the good. I then told everyone what happened to me on the way to the service, an event that Marian would have loved.

"I was riding here when I got a phone call from James Caan, the famous actor," I said. I explained that I have a client who knows Caan. So the call wasn't entirely unexpected.

My mobile phone rang and I heard the famous voice say, "Joe, this is Jimmy Caan."

"Oh my G—"

"What are you doing?" he asked.

"Well, ah, I'm going to a funeral."

"A funeral?!"

"I lost my ex and best friend," I said.

"My condolences, but I'm glad it was your ex," he said, stressing the word *ex*, not knowing, of course, how Marian and I remained close even after we legally separated.

There was an awkward silence.

I was on the phone with a celebrity, a man now 64 years old, still vibrant with life, starring in a weekly TV show called *Las Vegas*. I wanted more. I thought maybe he could offer something wise to help ease my pain. So far I had found no magic bullets, magic pills, magic words, books, or anything else to ease the grief.

"Do you have any advice for me?" I asked.

"Advice!?" he asked, surprised. "You don't want any advice from me. I've got a lot of ex wives, and some of them I wish would trade places with your ex."

I laughed out loud.

I told everyone at the service about this event, and they laughed, too.

And suddenly I realized that a miracle had taken place.

"Marian said it's all good," I told the people at the service. "She loved movies and loved *The Godfather*. The fact that I spoke with James Caan today, on the day of her service, would have made her smile that contagious huge beaming smile of hers. Marian knew the secret of the universe before me and most anyone else."

I broke into tears and said, "It's been four days of pure hell, with my missing her in the most painful ways, but on some level, in some way that I don't yet understand, this is all good."

That was all last night. The service is over. Marian is gone.

What I dislike about death is that it is so final. There is no P.S., no follow-up, and no chance to say hello, goodbye, I'm sorry, or I love you, or anything else. None. Zip. Zero. Game over. Plug pulled. The end.

Oh, you can play mind games and have conversations in your head with the deceased, but the person—the flesh and blood person who you knew and loved and could touch and hold—is gone.

My advice to you, and to me, is to live now. Be sure your affairs are in order—have a legal will, make peace with family and friends every day—and look for the good in every moment. It may not be easy, at first, but you can do it.

For example, a friend called me the other day, to see how I was handling the loss. We spoke for a while. He shared his own feelings of sadness. He told me, "It's real easy to fall into negative thinking."

I agreed, but I thought about it and realized I wasn't falling into negative thinking. I'm grieving. I'm sad. I'm at times barely able to function, but I'm not thinking negatively. Along the way in my life with Marian, I learned that "It's all good." Even the grieving. Even death.

When we drove back home from Houston today, traffic suddenly stopped. We didn't know what happened. Then we saw a helicopter, and knew someone was badly hurt and being carried to a hospital. As traffic moved again, we were able to see that a terrible wreck had taken place.

Moments before it happened, the drivers were talking, laughing, maybe planning their evening. Now they're hurt and possibly dead.

You never know what moment is our last one. I suggest you live now.

I suggest when opportunities come your way, grab them. I suggest you do more smiling, hugging, sharing, crying, laughing, risking, and forgiving. I suggest you monitor your thoughts, notice the negative ones, and consciously replace them with positive ones.

Yes, I know it can be difficult, at first. I've learned, from the Mental Toughness Institute's program that I'm in, that your thoughts can be elevated. You can rise above negative thinking. You simply have to retrain your brain. You have the power to do it. You just might need some support to make it your new habit.

Well, Marian pointed the way.

She said, "It's all good."

This is the one and only moment of your life.

It's the only moment you can count on.

This is it.

And it's good.

❦

The Healer's Secret—How Can This Secret Transform Your Relationships?
William Wittmann, M.Ed., LMP

My mother introduced me to one of the most powerful mysteries that any healer can be given. It is, in fact, the secret that underlies all my healing work. Although this mystery was revealed to me at age 8, it continues to deepen over the decades.

Travel back with me to the mid 1950s. World War II was still influencing everything. My parents and all my friends' parents had been involved in the war—their generation called it "the war" for the remainder of their lives. John Wayne's war movies were omnipresent on the black and white TVs. Guns and war were part of the fabric of life. War was still good.

My first bank account was in Sandy Springs, Maryland. Quakers owned and operated the bank. Behind the bank was the Quaker Meeting House where my mother and her family attended, and where I was sometimes obliged to go. Once a summer we underwent the ordeal of having to attend.

Now to the meat.

"Mom," I asked, "How come the bank guards don't carry guns?" My imagined reality contained cops and robbers, and I had noticed this disparity. I was concerned for my life's savings, which were on deposit.

After pausing a beat, she honored me with a real answer, "Well, Quakers believe that there is that of Christ in everyone."

. . . And I got it!

It is amazing these words penetrated my Indian killing, Alamo defending, Davy Crocket infused brain.

I understood, "If you think the other guy has Christ in them, you don't want to shoot them because you don't want to shoot Christ." This all made exquisite sense to me.

There Is That Of Christ In Everyone.

—Margaret Wittmann, Mom

An Ecumenical Pause

I was raised with Christian traditions, and I am comfortable with them, but I want to assure you that I have found all of the principles in this chapter in many other traditions. They are neither original nor unique to Christianity.

I prefer not to use Christian terminology with my clients because most have too many fuzzy doctrines lying about their minds gathered from years of exposure. Most of my patients are not Buddhists, so I use that language because it is unburdened by their personal history. I haven't met anyone with a negative Buddhist prejudice. Buddhist terminology is fresh for most clients.

Here's another truth I wish I had learned earlier:

> **Enlightened teachers of all traditions say the same thing.**

How Is "There Is That of Christ in Everyone" Useful?

Most doctors think of people as their complaint, conditions, and diseases.   It is easy to fall into this trap. We humans like to categorize and label:

- The kidney patient in room 305.
- The manic-depressive patient I saw yesterday.
- The old woman in my office.

As a healer, the minute I get conned into thinking of people as their disease or their condition, I lose my effectiveness. If I fall for their presenting symptoms and believe in their problems, all possibilities for healing disappear. They are doomed to live out the path of their disease or their condition.

As a healer, I work to see "that of Christ" in my patients. I say *work* because sometimes my patients present such engaging stories that I get caught up in the story, and I am even tempted to rescue them.

However, when I remember they are Christ or Buddha or Beings of White Light, then no rescue is required. I then bring my 30+ years of skills to bear on the problems at hand to help and support the Wondrous Being inside. "No worries," as our Australian friends say.

We don't discard our worldly skills; we harness them to these insights. When we harness the insight to the skills, the work becomes much easier with the possibility of staggering breakthroughs.

Potent Healing Idea—Go into Cahoots

I serve my patients best when I go into cahoots with the Christ in them to work on their problems.

For where two or three are gathered together in my name, there am I in the midst of them.

—MATTHEW 18:20

This teaching builds on your knowing that "there is that of Christ in everyone." When we align ourselves with that profound spiritual nature, miracles can occur.

Imagine how confident you would be if you knew *your* work were in alignment with the sacred. Possibilities occur that would not have occurred when we just look at the normal disease prognosis.

So, the Christ in me goes into cahoots with the Christ in them and healing happens, possibilities unfold, the world changes.

When I touch patients during my hands-on work, I contact the sacred, the ancestor, and the ancient wisdom in them. This wisdom knows how to heal. I just listen and follow directions.

I would have liked to know the implications of this at a deeper level at a much earlier time, but I won't complain. It may take a lifetime to unfold this kind of wisdom.

Seeing "that of Christ" in people has been the core of my success with patients and students for years.

"But, William, I Am Not a Healer, How Does This Help Me?"

Well, first of all, we are all healers and teachers, right? But let's put that aside.

You are in relationships with other people all day. When you apply the insight that "there is that of Christ in everyone" to your relationships, they will be transformed magnificently.

Imagine what it would be like if all the people in your life were enlightened beings. What would your life look like?

Clerks in stores become saints, servers in restaurants become holy teachers, and your loved ones become magical.

The Power of Expectation

What would happen if you expected everyone you know and those you come into contact with to be enlightened? What if you held them to a standard of excellence? The evidence in studies with children and teachers is clear.

If you take a class of average students and tell the teacher that this is a class of exceptionally bright kids with high IQs, the students perform better and their scores on IQ tests at the end of the year go up. The opposite also happens.

Our expectations affect what we get in the world.

Expect enlightened souls, and you live in heaven. No kidding.

This is a good world to live in.

May you be so blessed.

William Wittman is a body therapist. See www.vitalarts.net.

❧

Three Secrets
Marc Gitterle, M.D.

Faith is essential to prayer; we have all heard that axiom in some form or other. In fact, you might recall the great parable about prayer: "all it takes is a mustard seed . . ." What most of us forget is the second half of the parable (paraphrased): "therefore, pray that you will have that mustard seed of faith."

Huh? Let me sum it up: it doesn't take much faith to succeed at prayer, but you probably don't have even that little bit. "Wow," you may be thinking, "nobody ever told me that! I thought we all had at least a tiny mustard seed of faith?"

The fact is, in my experience, most of us don't have enough faith. I'll venture to bet that you never connected with that fact before, but if you can embrace it now, your life will never be the same. For the few who discover faith, this is a life-remaking secret. It is one that can lay hidden in plain sight, if you will, for a lifetime.

You can access this truth, right now. Pray for a mustard seed of faith to begin growing inside you. Pray that faith will quickly grow in you and flourish, so that your prayers are empowered and become effective. You will not feel any different, but you will be in possession of something invisible and awesomely powerful, right now, something no one can take from you. This something will grow inside you. Before long, it will become obvious to everyone who knows you well that something is different. I am not talking about religious concepts. Faith has *nothing* to do with religion. Religion co-opted faith, which was here long before.

Now that you have prayed for faith, it is time to embrace a second secret of prayer. Most people pray for embarrassingly tiny things. Why? The creative power of the universe has been listening to your prayers all your life and has been ready to make sweeping, dramatic changes to bless you and those whom you care for. However, we almost universally pray for miniscule things such as a slightly better job, for our marriage to become a little better (people have prayed that their marriage would be bearable!), to make a little more money. Instead, why not pray brashly? I have it on good authority that this is the way to do it.

You can start right now: I suggest that you pray that your income will increase dramatically. Go for it. I recommend it! And then, why not pray for your relationships to be amazing? Not just okay! Pray in rich detail for gems like this: "I pray that I be an incredible husband (or wife), delighting my spouse with romance, strength, solace, and deep, sweet friendship." If you are not married and want to be, why not pray that you will be in a romance of storybook intensity, and that it will lead to an enduring marriage full of more romance, happiness, mutual personal growth, and adventure.

Why not transform your workplace? How about praying that you will bless immensely the people you work with and that you find delight in working with them, and that you will be a catalyst of creativity, wisdom, and that people will find you a delight to work with. Pray that you will work for an incredible and enlightened company that will push the envelope for positive and dramatic change in their sphere of business.

The theme is obvious. It is just as easy for the creative force that creates the universe (and recreates it each instant!) to do great and wonderful things in response to your prayers as it is to do miniscule things. Prayer is a creative partnership between your will and vision and the creative power of the designer of the universe. You are truly called, I believe, to co-create in every area of your life. As Joe Vitale says, *Aude liquid dignum*! Dare something worthy.

Well, I am suggesting that *every day*, you dare something great in prayer. Why not? In fact, every time you see something that underwhelms you in any way—be it in the mirror, across the room, on the news—why not pray for it to be transformed into something great?

Now, here is another secret that will truly empower all your prayers. After you know what you want to pray in your head, send it with feeling, from your *heart center*, right in the middle of your chest. That is where real prayers come from, not from your head! You are now in possession of one of the most closely guarded secrets of life. Yes, real prayers are formulated in the mind, and sent from the heart. It is a beautiful partnership, and it works. It is the way we were made to function. Try it, right now. You will know that it is different from the old way of doing things, immediately. In fact, you will soon experience something really amazing; you will simply *know* your prayer has been answered immediately, as your prayer is being sent off, by your heart. That doesn't mean that you will see the answer immediately; rather, you will have a sense of knowing it will become reality. The rest is just a bit of time and watching details unfold.

Finally, I will present a third secret, which, when combined with the others, will lead you into such revolutionary change you will be smiling years from now as you look back on a life changed by prayer so dramatically that it is virtually unrecognizable. That secret is this: when you send off a prayer, *let it go*. Smile, sigh a sigh of release, and let it go. Let it fly to heaven like a small bird on graceful wings. If you continue to feel a sense of unease in your chest, as though you have not let it go, then you haven't let it go. Like a bird tethered to its perch, that prayer cannot reach heaven if your heart is holding on to it. Let go and let it soar. *Smile, and let it soar.*

One additional secret: because you are in direct contact with the designer of the universe, why not pray often for the most precious things of all, namely, that you will be continually *transformed* fully into a truly wise, truly loving, truly great human being, who spreads joy, faith, hope, and love contagiously. This is not some corny sentiment. This is the real deal. This is not just a possibility; it will be a living reality if you simply dare to pray for these truly great things. However, we are here to live all of life, so do not think for a minute that you should not be praying for any thing good that you really want, be that a really amazing car, a beautiful relationship, or that house on the beach in Maui. Praying for anything that is dear to you is an act of engaging intimately and dynamically with the creator of all these great things. It is an act of acknowledgment of that creative power and love that brought yourself into being.

As I look back at more than a decade of my life since I began my adventure of applying these incredible secrets, I see *revolution* in every area: marriage, career, friendships, creativity, leisure, learning. Virtually from the time I get up in the morning until I go to sleep at night, I am surrounded by often improbably, astonishingly, amazing answered prayers.

———

Dr. Marc Gitterle is coauthor of a forthcoming book, *No Effort Healing.*

ASSEMBLY REQUIRED

❧

Creating Your Future

Almost All First Steps Are Awkward

You may not remember, but your first steps were awkward.

You fell down a lot. You probably bumped your head. You may have scraped a knee, but you got up. You learned to walk. You learned to run. You made it to here.

Well done.

The same way you learned to walk is how you learn to do anything.

Take some stabs at it. Walk a little, wobble, fall down. Get up again.

That's the real secret: Get up again.

As long as you get up again, you're never out of life.

Don't Fall Back
Bill Hibbler

I've been an entrepreneur for as long as I can remember. When I was a kid, I sold newspaper subscriptions and even toothbrushes door to door. Later I had a paper route.

When I got interested in rock and roll, I started creating music businesses.

At age 15, I was renting out sound systems for special events and selling vintage guitars to all the big bands that came through Houston. At the time, I didn't care that much about making money but loved getting backstage to meet my favorite rock stars.

I worked with everyone from Aerosmith to Chuck Berry to Muddy Waters to ZZ Top. Name the band, I probably sold them a guitar or some gear.

While backstage, I'd watch the roadies setting up and tearing down the gear, doing all the little things it takes to move a rock band from city to city. And I knew exactly what I wanted to be when I grew up.

The rock stars were fun to watch onstage but not necessarily that impressive offstage. The person that impressed me the most was the road manager.

The road manager ran the show. He was responsible for making sure everyone is where they're supposed to be when they're supposed to be. If there was a problem, he solved it, and a good road manager runs things as tight as any military operation.

And what a lifestyle.

The road manager could wear his hair as long as he wanted and could dress in jeans and T-shirt (leather jacket optional). He seemed to get more girls than even the band did. As you might imagine, this appealed to me.

My parents didn't share my enthusiasm. In fact, they were horrified. It never occured to them that my building business relationships with rock stars at such a young age showed some potential for success in music.

"You need to go to college," they told me. I told them they didn't teach how to be a road manager in college. "You need to go and get your degree first, then if you still want to, go do your rock and roll thing. That way, you'll have something to fall back on."

Would you believe I listened to them?

In the fall of 1977, I enrolled in the University of Houston as an accounting major. Six weeks later, I dropped out. College was not for me.

Back then, there were no books on how to be a road manager. What I really needed was a mentor, but I had no idea how to find one.

This was back in the days before voice mail, cell phones, and e-mail. I'd meet road managers at the shows but they'd usually be too busy to stop and talk for any length of time.

Because of their attitude toward the music biz, I couldn't talk to my parents. If I voiced doubts about what I was doing or a particular situation, they saw that as an opportunity to discourage me from continuing.

They didn't do much to help my confidence. And they were always on and on with that "You need something to fall back on." As a result, I shut them out of my life and they did the same. (We eventually made peace several years later).

Despite the lack of support, at the ripe old age of 22, I became the road manager for the British band Humble Pie. I toured the United States several times over the next few years until the band broke up and the members returned to England.

I wore a lot of hats in the music biz, touring the world several times, and eventually ended up managing several artists. I retired from the music biz in 1998 and have since moved into Internet marketing, which I love almost as much as I did the music biz.

Although I had some success in music, I always felt a little crippled from the lack of support from my family. Far too often, I heard their voices in my head saying, "You need something to fall back on."

If there's one thing I've learned today it is that needing something to fall back on is a load of *bull*.

Having something to fall back on only guarantees one thing, you *will* fall back. It's far better to commit 100 percent to reaching your goals.

In the early 1500s, the Spanish explorer Cortez landed at the southeast coast of Mexico. He ordered his men to remove all the sails, metal fittings, and cannons from the ship. He then ordered his men to burn the ships so there could be no retreat.

By burning those ships, Cortez committed himself and his men to face an unknown continent knowing they might never see Spain again. They had nothing to fall back on.

Did he succeed? Well, there's a reason they speak Spanish in Mexico.

If you want to fulfill your dreams, whatever they may be, you've got to be willing to burn your ships, and you've got to be willing to do whatever it takes.

If you have children, encourage them to follow their dreams, even if they aren't exactly what you had in mind for them.

And never tell them they need something to fall back on.

———

Bill Hibbler is a famous Internet marketer. See www.Ecommerce Confidential.com.

❦

A New Way to Easily Achieve Your Goals

I've learned at least two things about achieving goals: There is an easy way and a hard way.

The hard way is to work night and day, stay obsessed, rarely sleep, and never give up.

Because everyone talks about the hard way, I want to address the easy way. After all, why struggle if you don't have to?

I've used the easy way to create bestselling books, lose 70 pounds in 8 months, find my ideal mate, get healthy, increase my wealth, and much more.

Obviously, it works.

Here's the formula in brief:

- Be grateful for what you already have.
- Playfully declare what you would like to have with positive emotion, feeling as if it is already achieved.
- Act on the nudges and opportunities that appear.

That's it. In my latest book, *The Attractor Factor*, I explain a five-step formula for getting what you want. It's useful for those times when you don't feel grateful, or can't decide on what you want, or don't understand the concept of letting go while taking inspired action. It's also helpful when you have issues about money, or deserving, or feel in any way blocked from your goals.

However, the bottom line for me is this: Declare what you would like with no attachment and plenty of good feeling, feel grateful for what you already have, and act on what appears. The result will be a happy life.

Let's explore this in depth.

Feel Grateful Now

It doesn't mater where you live or what you have. If you're reading this, you're most likely living like a king or queen compared to people in third world countries. You may even be living better than kings or queens from history, as they often lived in cold, violent, frightful times. You've got it made.

Choose What You Want Without Attachment, Feeling as if It Is Already Achieved

There's magic in saying "I'd love to _____ (fill in the blank), but I won't die if I don't have it." Because the world is simply energy taking form, when you declare you want something, you begin to attract it. However, when you say you need something, the need pushes it away. You want to select your desire, and feel the joy of already having it, without feeling any desperation. Need will push it away; desire will attract it. If you feel as if you already have your desire, then you will have it.

Act on Your Opportunities and Intuitions

You may get offers, calls, or who knows what. Act on them. You never know what will lead you to your goal. Your ego cannot see the big picture. Intuition and opportunities will come to you from the larger view, and your job is to act on them. As you do, you will be taken to your goal, even when it appears you are being blocked from it.

Trust is Key

Is that really all there is to it?

Again, the fuller procedure in *The Attractor Factor* will take care of any snags in the process, but the basic process is simple. Let's walk through the three steps:

1. Look around your room. What are you grateful for? Make a list. Get into the authentic feeling of true gratitude. In other words, be happy now. You don't need a reason to be happy, but if you want one, find something, anything, to be grateful for right now. When you're grateful, you're in a mental place that will attract more to be grateful for.

2. Look around the playground of your mind. What would you like to have, do, or be? What would be fun? Write it down. As you do, feel what it would be like to already have it now. Pretend you won the lotto. What would you want for yourself or others? What would be fun? The key is playful nonattachment while experiencing its completion *now*.

3. Now pay attention. As you go about your life, listen to your hunches and act on them, and pay attention to the opportunities and act on them. You never know what will take you in the direction of your goal. Your job is to take inspired action. You may have some work to do in this step, but the work will be from your heart, and will take you in the direction of getting your goal.

Why not go through the steps right now?

Write them down, experience them, and then check back in a few weeks and see how they are doing. You may surprise yourself by how easily and quickly your goals are achieved.

If you find yourself doubting the process, thinking negatively, or in any way not enjoying the simplicity of the easy way to attain your goals, then consider learning the five-step process in *The Attractor Factor*.

Above all, have fun. Keep smiling. Be playful. Stay grateful. These are all elements of the new secret to manifesting your goals.

Remember the words of a famous song that also perfectly summarizes this new way to achieve your goals: "Don't Worry. Be Happy."

〜

Spinning the Roulette Wheel to Self-Fulfillment
Dr. Rick Barrett

The most precious gem that I could pass on to others to enrich their lives can be summed up in one small yet powerful word—**service**.

To pursue a life of giving to others enables us to learn, grow, and appreciate. We become empowered and open to receiving even greater rewards for ourselves.

Serving others is to the soul what food and water is to the body. It not only sustains us but allows us to reach our full potential, experience high levels of performance, and ultimately attain great riches, spiritually and materially. Had I known that I could satisfy all my needs and be rewarded in this life and potentially in the next, I certainly would have begun at the earliest possible age.

Learning proper investing techniques at a later age simply means that your outcome will be limited. However, learning simple investing strategies as a child can create massive financial reward over a lifetime. So, too, with serving others. How much reward can be attained with simply serving others on a regular basis? I believe it is unlimited!

When I was young, I had the limited belief that helping others was to be done by donating money to other people whose jobs it was to serve. Monetary donations are fine and wonderful, but usually they are minimal and never stretch a person. Much like exercising, if all you ever do is an occasional (whenever you feel like it) push up or sit up, you will never make an impact, never producing a result of increased health, weight loss, or an improved body. Likely you will not feel any different. In other words, it is a weak attempt, and there is no reward. However, if you stretch yourself, work out rigorously with a plan, with regularity, you will see and feel a massive change. You will be the recipient of a great reward!

Giving and serving is much like that. Yes, a few dollars here and there helps someone, but it is like a teardrop in the ocean. It goes unnoticed and creates no change. Giving large sums of money with regularity can and will make a change. Certainly rewards will be brought your way, but to really stretch your soul to expand goodness and to open yourself to more abundance, there is no substitute for personal service involvement!

Most people, including myself, develop an inward-focused mind posture. This mind posture sets us up to believe that life is all about ourselves and that we each have the right to suck out anything we want that this planet has to offer. This is the very opposite to the thinking of some groups like Native Americans who believe that we are all part of the earth, the sky, the animals, and we must only use what we absolutely need. Don't waste and don't overindulge. It is the difference between being selfish or selfless.

The truth is life isn't all about selfishness! It's about others. Everything I desire and need can be mine if I choose to focus on giving to others. To become a servant of others allows us to grow exponentially in every area of our lives and, I believe, into our future spiritual lives. Certainly it's normal to desire and strive to have and accumulate certain things in our lives, but by focusing all the energy inwardly on oneself with the idea of getting as much as we can and maybe giving a little bit away is not only selfish but limiting, not only to others but to ourselves. Unfortunately, it seems to be the norm in our society. What should be the norm, and I believe to be a better course of action, is helping others achieve and get as much as they can and keeping a little for ourselves. By this mechanism, many benefit. The greater the good that is done for others then can be returned and multiplied many times over.

I am sure you have seen pictures of both explosions and implosions. An implosion directs its energy inwardly. The videos of a building being imploded are magnificent. The charges go off and the whole building crumbles inwardly to the ground in a rather tight circumference of debris. But an explosion, like an atomic blast, forces it's energy outward creating massive destruction over great distances. Both an implosion and an explosion are destructive forces, but take the idea of it and think of a positive explosion of energy. Would you rather be an explosive positive energy force that affects untold numbers of people including you and the planet or a small implosive device with a limited impact? Personally I want to be explosive and do more, not only for my family and myself, but I'd like to make the biggest impact on the planet that a human being can possibly make. This can be done by maintaining a focus on service and outward attention to others. This is what needs to be part of the guide book we are given at birth and taught to implement as soon as we have the ability to understand.

Envision the end of your life. If you had the opportunity before you died to reflect on your life, would the reflection be beautiful and abundant or would it be ugly and desolate? The question is how will we be judged by ourselves, humanity, and God? How do we want to be remembered? Did we make a positive substantial difference in people's lives? Or did we squander our lives and ignore our opportunities to help humanity?

Of course we all tend to believe we will live long lives with plenty of time to accomplish what we want, but reality can be quite different. Life, at least our human tangible form, is truly fleeting. We aren't privileged to know how much time we have on this planet. The roulette wheel of life spins and the ball lands on different numbers for all of us, and we are unable to know which number it will be or to influence it. For one person it might be 101, for another 25, and yet for another only 10. Knowing, then, not the actual number of our days but the absolute certainty that there is a number, shouldn't we act with the best intentions and for the greatest good on a daily basis? Each and every day builds on the last until the last day is reached.

It seems I am reminded of this almost on a daily basis. This past weekend I encountered death twice. The first time from a phone call on Saturday from one of my patients who informed me that her husband passed away. He was also my patient, and I have been blessed to have them as patients for over ten years. A World War II and Korean War veteran who had lost the battle to cancer, he was 81 years old. I attended his funeral on Monday.

The second encounter occurred as my wife and I were driving home on Sunday evening in the hills outside Austin, Texas. We happened upon the scene of an accident. We didn't see the accident, but we couldn't have been more than twenty seconds behind the impact as a few cars on each side of the road were just pulling to the shoulders. As I stopped my vehicle and rushed to lend assistance, a man was bending over the mangled body of a motorcyclist lying in the middle of the road. The scene is too gruesome to describe. As I reached them, the man told me he was a physician, he had checked for a pulse and the motorcyclist was dead. As I looked at the motorcyclist, it was clear from his head injury that he was, in fact, dead. It was hard to determine his age, but he was a young man. I thought how sad it was to be gone so young and I hoped he didn't have a wife and children that would have to be told of his fate. It was, once again, a vivid reminder that none of us knows how long his or her residence on this planet will last. The roulette wheel stopped on 81 for my patient, Dan, and a much lower number for this poor accident victim.

Immediately my thoughts ran to how much time I have left and whether I am doing enough. Am I satisfied with all that I accomplished and will I be leaving the planet, at least for some, better than when I came to it?

As I write this, I am making plans for more medical missionary trips, writing more books to help others, and a myriad of other things. Though you didn't receive this instruction manual when you were a child, it's never too late to start. Reflect on how you can start giving more and serving more. Create lists, get your spouse involved, get your children involved. Make today the beginning of a new era of serving, and start on the road to great reward. Serving others is like exercise; you can never do enough.

A parting gift I have for you is a simple prayer I created for my book, *Healed By Morning*. I hope it serves you well.

Lord God you are my creator.
I love you.
I am part of you, therefore, I cannot fail because you cannot fail.
I am capable of everything.
Ultimate health, happiness and success because I am part of
    you, and you are completely capable.
Every good wish I have, I can have, because you wish it for me.
I will not linger in darkness and doubt, because the spirit of your
    light illuminates my way.
You are in me and I am one with you.
Together we can accomplish miracles.

———

Dr. Rick Barrett is the author of numerous books, including *Dare to Break through the Pain.*

∽

The Top 10 Destructive Money Beliefs
(and How to Overcome Them)
Dan Klatt

If you're not making as much money as you'd like, then you're holding onto some negative beliefs about yourself and how much money you're capable of handling. In this article, we'll go through 10 of the most common (and most limiting) examples of how people hold themselves back financially. Subscribers to my e-zine, *The Abundant Mind*, get a Money Beliefs Quiz. From their results I've compiled these top 10 destructive money beliefs. How many can you relate to?

10. *Money is not spiritual.* This is the belief that you're somehow more spiritual or more likely to have a better afterlife if you sacrifice greatly this time around. Or that you'll suffer after you die if you pursue the things you want, which you need money to buy. This belief is most often an effect of people's religious upbringing. Remember, you're here to live life fully right now. (Also see belief 1.)

9. *I'll get to it tomorrow.* When you put things off, you step out of the natural flow which includes allowing abundance to come into your life. It's almost always based on your fear that you'll fail anyway, and that will disappoint you, so you delay what you feel is inevitable. Once you start living in the moment, though, you let go of the grip in which the past held you. You realize you're a new person now. You've learned and grown a lot since the last time things didn't go as planned (and that only happened because you still had not learned something you needed then to succeed, which you probably know now).

8. *I'll probably just fail anyway.* We've probably all heard the wisdom of Wayne Gretzky: "You always miss the shot you don't take." When people don't take action because they're afraid they'll fail, well, guess what, by not even trying they

already have failed. You have already succeeded just by moving forward. You may not achieve your objectives right away, yet you will still have learned some valuable lessons. And that makes it more likely you'll succeed next time.

7. *But we can't afford that.* This kind of thinking comes from scarcity and lack, not abundance. It also gets people to focus on what they don't have (which empowers them not having). They feel as though the things they do have are not enough. Instead, when you appreciate everything you do have, you come from a mindset of abundance and start bringing the things you want closer to you. You also realize there is no limit to what you can become, accomplish, or have.

6. *Rich people are greedy and dishonest.* The first person to spread this untruth must have been a poor person. The fact is that most people who become wealthy are at least somewhat aware of the spiritual principles that allowed them to prosper. A key part of that is to stay in the flow, which means giving back. Rich people are among the most generous, too, and they started their habit of giving long before they started having a lot of money. Coincidence? Not a chance.

5. *If I'm successful, my friends will be jealous and stop liking me.* Remember that we live in an abundant universe. There *is* enough for everyone. People who envy what others have are coming from scarcity and actually are a harmful influence on your abundant mind. It's actually critical to your experience of prosperity to only allow positive, supportive, and inspiring messages into your brain, and that especially includes your own thoughts!

4. *I'm no better than my parents, so I shouldn't make more than they did.* The world was much different when your parents were where you're at. Tools like the Internet have made it possible for everyone to make a lot of money doing what they love. Besides, your parents may have struggled precisely to give you a better life than they had. They loved you and would want it no other way.

3. *I might forget what's truly important and not like the person I've become.* People who are greedy still come from scarcity and lack, and if they made lots of money, they will not enjoy it and are more likely to lose it). Instead, you come from a mindset of abundance, and you know that encompasses far more than material wealth. In fact, it requires a balance between great health, meaningful relationships, ample time for relaxation and playing, and truly enjoying your financial abundance. You will have an abundance of happiness when you come from an abundant mind.

2. *Money is the root of all evil.* This is the most common error we learn from our parents and religious institutions, and it keeps millions in poverty and a slave to money. That, by the way, is the only way we may judge money as "evil"— when it controls us. And that only happens when we feel we need it, because we're coming from scarcity and lack. When you come from abundance, money becomes a tool to enjoy the finer things in life and to give you everything you need to fulfill your life purpose. That's why we're here, right?

1. *I'm not worthy.* Do you realize that fully 90 percent of the population has an issue with low self-esteem? It's the number one thing that holds people back and prevents them from living their dreams. When people feel they don't deserve wealth or abundance in any area, they don't take the opportunities they're given. Instead, they do nothing and complain about others who have become abundant. They also make up lots of excuses to justify how life has done them wrong. Instead, please realize that the abundant mind is what separates the richest person from the crowd, and you can choose right now to come from abundance and take your place among the wealthy. You are worthy.

———

Dan Klatt created the Inner Wealth Mastery Program through http://tinyurl.com/fjfd.

❦

Your Mind Is an Instrument for Poverty or Prosperity
Randy Gage

This is either the scariest thing you will ever hear, or the most liberating insight you will ever learn. Make it the latter, and you are well on your way to abundance.

No two people ever view the same event in the same way. Where one may see a threat, the other sees opportunity. Suppose you are offered a chance to participate in a business opportunity. You could approach this in a number of different ways.

You could jump in blindly, without doing any research, just because you are enamored with the idea of getting rich. This could bring you to a very bad situation, and you could lose a lot of money.

Or, scenario two, you could figure that any deal you find out about is already too late. You could think that the insiders get all the sweetheart deals, and it's probably much too good to be true, so you pass up the chance to buy IBM when it is $10 a share.

Another scenario might occur when you get offered a situation, you have confidence in yourself, you study it thoroughly, and, you make a sound decision. How you will react to the opportunity is determined almost entirely by your mindset, which reflects what you expect from life. Of all the tools you can use to manifest your prosperity, your mind is the most powerful.

———

Randy Gage is the author of the best-selling albums, *Dynamic Development* and *Prosperity* and director of www.BreakthroughU.com. For more resources and to subscribe to Randy's free e-zine newsletters visit http://www.MyProsperitySecrets.com.

❦

When Bad Things Happen to Good People

What looks horrible in the moment usually looks good a few years from now.

I remember reading a helpful passage in one of my favorite books, *Breaking the Rules* by Kurt Wright. It goes like this:

*Have you ever noticed how easy it is to look back on events
that happened a year or more in the past and see the perfection
in them? For most of us this is true even for situations which
seemed tragic, horrible or even devastating at the time. Now,
if it is possible to see the perfection in those things a year later,
doesn't it make sense that the perfection must be there in the
moment it happens, too?*

With that in mind, see if you can get some positive perspective
on any bad event right now.

Ask yourself, "What are some positive things that could come
from this event?"

Cancer survivor Lance Armstrong ended up saying that cancer
was the best thing that ever happened to him. Without it, he said he
would never have been motivated to win the Tour de France.

Look for the good in the bad.

It's there.

❦

Everything You Do Will Be a Success

Everything you do in life will be a success.

You won't think so at times because you'll compare the reality of
what happened to the goal you intended to happen.

For example, if you wanted to lose 15 pounds but lost 10 pounds,
you'll call that a failure. But you actually succeeded at losing 10
pounds.

If you tried to start a business and made ten dollars and lost ten
thousand, you'll call it a failure. However, you learned what to do
and what not to do, so you had a successful education. And you
made ten bucks, to boot.

While you may always desire to achieve the goals you stated, always remind yourself that whatever the outcome, you succeeded in
some way.

Life is Short
Jillian Coleman

Like everybody else, I got a lot of advice growing up. I got it from my parents and my grandparents. I got it from the priests and the nuns at church and in grammar school, high school, and a Catholic university. I got it from the thousands of books I devoured, and hundreds of movies. I got it from the radio serials I listened to every week, like *Sergeant Preston of the Yukon* and *The Lone Ranger.* I got it from TV, from *Howdy Doody* and *Sky King* and *Roy Rogers.*

A lot of it was helpful, and a lot of it was worse than useless.

The older I get, the more I seem to return to the basics. My mother was right; sugar isn't good for you. My grandfather was right; it's important to save your money. The nuns were right; life is happier when I forgive those who've hurt me, and monogamy works better than sleeping around.

Of all the advice I ever received, the one counsel that has most influenced my life, the one I really took to heart and accepted as a guide, came from my father. He said, "Life is too short not to do what you want."

Well, that's how he said it when I was younger. Later on, I often heard the uncensored, R-rated version of: "Life is too short to let anybody jerk you around."

It was hard living with my father when I was a kid. He'd been in the war, and it made him a little crazy. He was brilliant and charming, but also violent and unpredictable. He was more than a little sadistic. He was a complicated man who took a long time sorting himself out, and I spent a lot of years in therapy sorting out myself as a result. But that's another story, as they say.

My father didn't accept many of the conventional values, but he had strongly held values nevertheless. Loyalty was one, especially family loyalty. Intellectual curiosity was another. His most cherished value, however, was his commitment to his personal freedom. He lived life absolutely on his own terms.

My terms are different than my dad's. I've made different choices, and established different priorities. However, I have consistently lived my life to please myself, and done what I wanted to do.

My dad's advice has empowered me to work for myself. It has allowed me to walk away from an unhappy marriage (even though my father himself gave me a lot of grief over that decision). It has given me the strength to turn my back on false friends, and to stand up to authority. It has enabled me to question doctors, and it has taken me into the streets to protest racism and wars. It has encouraged me to live my life with courage, appetite, and adventure.

Today I sometimes refer to myself as middle-aged, but recently a friend teasingly pointed out to me that few people live to be a hundred and twenty. I am probably closer to the last third of my life than the last half. In many ways, I am mellower than I was 20 or 30 years ago. My father's advice still rings in my mind, and for however long I have left, I plan to live with this as my guide. Life is too short not to do what you want.

––––––

Jillian Coleman Wheeler is a Grants and Business Consultant to businesses and nonprofit organizations. Her web site, www.GrantMeRich.com, is a resource site for entrepreneurs, grant writers and consultants, and offers online training for grants consultants. She is also author of *The New American Land Rush: How to Buy Real Estate with Government Money*. For more information, visit www.NewAmericanLandRush.com.

⌐∿

The Owner's Manual I Wish I Had Gotten at Birth
Pat O'Bryan

–––––––––––––––––––––––––––––––––––––––

As soon as you're born, they make you feel small
By giving you no time, instead of it all . . .

—JOHN LENNON

–––––––––––––––––––––––––––––––––––––––

When I think of what I wish I had been told at birth, the answer is nothing. The people doing the telling were doing their best, I guess, but they got it all wrong.

Everything I was told was wrong. Everything you were told is probably wrong, too.

We come into this world with everything we need. We start losing that wisdom as soon as we start listening to parents, teachers, and the media.

Much of our formative years are spent learning the rules: the rules of grammar, the rules of deportment, the rules of polite society, the rules of success and happiness. Only after years of study and personal deconstruction have I learned the real truth about rules. There ain't no such thing. For winners, there ain't no rules.

Take the rules for success. I don't know about you, but I was told to study hard, do well in school, get a good job. That's the road to success.

If there is a better way *not* to be successful in this world, I don't know what it could be. And yet, parents, teachers, and other well-meaning people recited this rule to me over and over again. They're still reciting it.

Go ask Bill Gates if he wants a job. Go ask Steve Jobs if he wants a job. Go ask Richard Branson if he wants a job.

Go look at a list of the most successful people on the planet, and see how many of them have jobs.

Zero. Zip. Nada.

They create businesses. They create jobs. However, the most successful people on the planet have ideas. They don't have jobs.

How about education? Again, I can only relate to my personal experience, but my education made me highly qualified to sit at a desk and do rote tasks over and over again. My education would have been very useful if my ultimate goal had been to be a nineteenth-century factory worker.

I specifically do *not* want to be a nineteenth-century factory worker.

I want to be a twenty-first-century author, marketer, and entrepreneur. Where's the college for that?

The college where I got my diploma didn't have a Master of Entrepreneurship diploma. They offered a business degree. I got one.

It ain't worth the paper it's printed on and it's printed on some pretty cheap paper.

That college would have been glad to sell me a degree in English. I could study literature. Then I could be an author.

I'd like to ask a question, please. Why is the title failed, unpublished author a job prerequisite to teach writing at the college level?

I like to read. I like books. I'm a little skittish about literature.

Do you have to wear a tie when you read it? Can you read it in your underwear?

Is it okay to laugh at the silly bits? How can you read Charles Baudelaire, for example, without resorting to a belly laugh? I never could.

Of course, I never could pull off the black beret and turtleneck sweater, either. Apparently, that's what real writers wear.

I manage to be an author in spite of my education.

Education, at least as I experienced it, teaches all you need to know to fail completely, utterly completely. I don't know how other countries manage to create equally dramatic failures, if their educational system isn't as good as ours.

Wouldn't it be nice if there was a college diploma you could get in Success?

You'd start with Success 101—question everything—and end up at Success 499—create something of value.

Sign me up.

So, looking back, what kind of manual would I have liked to have had when I was born to help me achieve success in my life?

One that emphasized that you create the world you live in. We're making this up, you know.

One that emphasized that each person, including me, has to take responsibility for their life, and that, if that life isn't absolutely, deliriously blissful, then that person is authorized by the highest authority to change it.

I'd like a chapter on social norms, and what a ball and chain they can be if you let them. Miserable people want you to join them, but you can choose not to. If the invitation says, black tie, and you're feeling tie dye, go for it.

In the part of Texas I'm from, white cowboy hats must not be worn after Labor Day—you must wear your black one.

I say, be daring. Wear your white hat on Christmas Day, if you want to. If you're successful enough, you'll start a trend.

I want the manual to say, "Your job is to be outrageous, creative, and successful. And happy." That's it. End of story. All that work ethic stuff, guilt stuff, fear stuff, that's not for you. If you can be successful and happy by working one hour a year, go for it. It's okay with the universe.

At the end of the manual, a certificate, a nice one, with an embossed gold seal, saying:

> **You are hereby authorized to do whatever you feel you have the guts to try. You are hereby notified that you don't ever have to ask anyone else's permission to be successful or happy at anything.**
>
> **If you think you can do it, do it. You're authorized, by the power vested in your own soul, as evidenced by this certificate, to live your dreams to the max. Now.**

I'd mount that certificate on the wall, proudly. Wouldn't you? What's this got to do with success?

Most people are failures, aren't they? They work all week at a job they hate, for their entire lives and then try to forget who they are for the weekend, until they go back to the job they hate on Monday morning. Most people really do lead lives of quiet desperation, and then die without having ever lived.

If you do what most people do, you'll get the results most people get.

If you want something other than the obvious to happen, you need to do something other than the obvious. And you need to do it now.

———

Pat O'Bryan is an internationally famous blues guitarist and Internet marketing celebrity. See www.PatOBryan.com.

*Only you can diminish your self-esteem and only you can
restore it. Freedom comes with non-attachment to whatever
another says or does.*

—Dr. Joe Rubino

 ∽

Aude aliquid dignum

I discovered a sixteenth-century Latin phrase that speaks to the
whole issue of goal setting: *Aude aliquid dignum.* It translates to
mean "Dare something worthy."

Ah! How it conjures up the noblest within us.

When you think about daring something worthy, you get past
your ego and your limitations. You start to think of the world and
helping others.

Some people have the goal of losing a few pounds, or making
more money, or getting a raise or a new job. Those are all valid
goals.

But a goal that dares something worthy will be bigger. It might
be to achieve the all time fitness level for you. Or to break all known
records for your business. Or to start and achieve a dream that affects the planet.

When you dare something worthy, you tap into all the energy
within yourself, and you align yourself with the universe's desire to
grow.

Dare something worthy and you unlock the powers of yourself
and all that is.

Dare something worthy and you feel your heart sing.

Dare something worthy.

Today.

ABOUT THE AUTHOR

PHOTO BY JULIE ESKOFF

Dr. Joe Vitale, president of Hypnotic Marketing, Inc., located outside of Austin, Texas, is the author of way too many books to list here. Here are just a few of them:

He wrote the number-one bestseller, *The Attractor Factor: 5 Easy Steps for Creating Wealth (or anything else) from the Inside Out*, the number-three bestseller *The Greatest Money-Making Secret in History*, and the number-one best-selling E-book *Hypnotic Writing*. His latest book, written with Jo Han Mok, is *The E-Code: 33 Internet Superstars Reveal 43 Ways to Make Money Online Almost Instantly—with just e-mail.* His next book will be *There's a Customer Born Every Minute.*

Besides all of his books, Dr. Vitale also recorded the number-one best-selling Nightingale-Conant audio program, *The Power of Outrageous Marketing.* In addition, he has a complete home-study course in marketing at www.HypnoticMarketingStrategy.com.

Sign up for his complimentary newsletter *News You Can Use!* at his main web site at www.mrfire.com.